Wild Cherry:
Selected Poems

Nigel Jenkins (1949-2014) was one of Wales's leading writers: a poet and essayist, he was also a political activist, teacher, mentor, broadcaster, playwright, translator, psychogeographer and critic. Brought up on a farm on the Gower peninsula, he went on to study literature and film at Essex University and work as a journalist in England (via a brief stint as a circus roustabout in America). On his return to Wales in 1976 he learned Welsh and remained in Swansea, becoming a full-time writer and lecturer in Creative Writing.

His volumes of poetry include *Song and Dance* (1981), *Practical Dreams* (1983), *Acts of Union: Selected Poems 1974-1989* (1990), *Ambush* (1998), *Blue: 101 Haiku, Senryu and Tanka* (2002), *Hotel Gwales* (2006) and *O for a gun: 101 Haiku and Senryu* (2007). He co-edited *Another Country: Haiku Poetry from Wales* (2011) with Ken Jones and Lynne Rees.

Jenkins was elected to the Welsh Academy in 1978 and elected to the Gorsedd of Bards in 1998. He was a founder member, and later chairman, of the Welsh Union of Writers. Awards include a Welsh Arts Council's Young Poets Prize (1974), an Eric Gregory Award for poetry (1976), two Welsh Arts Council bursaries, the John Morgan Writing Award (1991), and the John Tripp Spoken Poetry Award (1998). He collaborated on works of public art with visual artists for Swansea City Council and the Ebbw Vale Garden Festival. He wrote two stage plays – *Strike a Light!* (1985) and *Waldo's Witness* (1986) and his critical biography of the poet John Tripp was published in 1989.

He was an accomplished writer of prose. In 1996, he won the Wales Book of the Year prize for his travel book *Gwalia in Khasia* (1995) – the story of the Welsh Calvinistic Methodists Mission to the Khasi Hills in north-east India (1841–1969). The book was accompanied by a BBC television film and a S4C documentary series, and an anthology of Khasi poetry and prose (*Khasia in Gwalia*, 1995). In 2001, he published a selection of his essays and articles as *Footsore on the Frontier* and, in 2008, his first psychogeographical guide book *Real Swansea* was published, followed by *Gower* (2009), *Real Swansea Two* (2012) and *Real Gower* (2014). He was a co-editor of the *Welsh Academy Encyclopaedia of Wales* (2008), and a noted translator from Welsh.

Jenkins was director of Swansea University's Masters programme in Creative Writing, on which he had taught since 2003. Much loved by his students, as a lecturer and tutor he worked for many organisations including Trinity College, Carmarthen, the Workers' Educational Association, and Tŷ Newydd, the National Writing Centre of Wales.

Wild Cherry:
Selected Poems

Nigel Jenkins

Edited by Patrick McGuinness

Parthian, Cardigan SA43 1ED www.parthianbooks.com
First published in 2023
© Estate of Nigel Jenkins 2023
ISBN 978-1-914595-22-6
Editor: Patrick McGuinness
Cover image: 'Map for Nigel', 2014, mixed media on handmade Indian Khadi paper by Iwan
Bala, 76 x 56 cm, Glynn Vivian Gallery, Swansea
Cover design by www.theundercard.co.uk
Typeset by Elaine Sharples
Printed and bound by 4edge Limited, UK
Published with the financial support of the Welsh Books Council
British Library Cataloguing in Publication Data
A cataloguing record for this book is available from the British Library
Printed on FSC accredited paper

Contents

from AMBUSH (1998)

from **O FOR A GUN (2007)**

Notes
Acknowledgments

Ambushed by Words

When Nigel Jenkins died at the age of sixty-four in 2014, he left behind a body of work remarkable not just for the range of its forms and occasions, but for the variety of its literary, cultural and political commitments.

The author of a groundbreaking book of travel-writing about the Welsh Calvinistic Mission in Khasi, North-East India, *Gwalia in Khasia,* which won the Wales Book of the Year in 1996, Jenkins wrote two books of ... what exactly – topography? history? psychogeography? – about the city he loved but never idealised: *Real Swansea* and *Real Swansea Two*. Published posthumously in the same series, and with the same breadth of knowledge, snappiness of phrasing and freshness of perspective, was *Real Gower* (2014), on which he had published, with the artist and photographer David Pearl, a richly-illustrated book in 2009. All three books also contain poems in and among the prose, as if to remind us that, for Jenkins, poetry and prose, far from being opposites, beget and sustain each other. These books are characterised by deep research, but also an understanding of how places and their histories are experienced in the here and now. This is reflected in the poetry Jenkins produced for public spaces in Swansea and elsewhere, where his words, executed in stone, steel, glass, and neon, adorn buildings and monuments, always arrestingly and without any trace of municipal committee-pleasing. His critical guide to the Welsh poet John Tripp appeared from the University of Wales Press in 1989, and a selection of essays on literature, place and culture, was published in 2001 as *Footsore on the Frontier*. The author of numerous books and pamphlets and the editor of several anthologies, Jenkins was also one of the editors, with John Davies, Menna Baines and Peredur Lynch, of the *Encyclopaedia of Wales / Gwyddoniadur Cymru*, which appeared in 2009.

I mention Jenkins's non-poetic writing in order to establish, from the start, the way his work centres itself in relation not just to Wales, its languages and its cultures, but to the world at large. Jenkins had a clear understanding of what it meant to be a Welsh poet writing in English in the 20th and 21st centuries. That understanding was informed and energised by its attentiveness to Welsh-language culture, and from its sense that the English-language tradition of Wales could learn from the centrality of poetry in Welsh-speaking society. Jenkins saw himself in the tradition of what he called, quoting Harri Webb, 'the poet as essentially a social rather than a solitary character'. And yet that is only one facet of his work, because Jenkins's poetry is also intimate and reflective, and though there are moments of solitude, there is never a retreat into private language.

'As we reappropriate some of the active principles of our native tradition, we need at the same time to be open to and avid of non-Welsh stimulation. More poetry from Asia, the Americas, Africa...', he argued in a talk given at the opening of Tŷ Llên in Swansea (now the Dylan Thomas Centre) in 1995. On the same occasion, he made the case for poetry's role in this 'reappropriation': 'Poetry should be out and about, doing a job in the world, ambushing people, not hiding in classroom cupboards and magazines that nobody reads'. Not for nothing did Jenkins title his 1998 volume *Ambush*: a one-word poetic manifesto, it was also a fitting description of the way in which his own poetry stakes its claim upon us.

In an interview with the magazine *Roundyhouse* in 2006, Jenkins described how, after a wounding review of his first poems, he returned to the family farm in Gower and started again. The poems in which, by his own estimation, he began to sound like himself are the ones that open this book. 'Pig-Killing Day', 'First Calving' and 'Castration' are visceral poems about the realities of farming life, conveyed in what Jenkins called 'the plain, ungarnished language' which he developed as a counterweight to the excesses of 'the Dylan Thomas imitation epoch'. The return to Gower was a grounding, or a re-grounding, and it was literal as well as metaphorical.

Jenkins's poetry is often concerned with grounding, but it is also a poetry of connection and connectiveness. For Jenkins, poetry must do more than merely express the romantic self or the atomised postmodern 'I'. He dismissed 'the poetry of demure ego, whimsical anecdote, genteel suburban regret and detail-obsessed imagism', and, like the poets he knew and admired in Welsh and English, Jenkins wrote with Wales in mind. The Wales he wrote from, and wrote *towards*, was not some abstract idea, but a living place, imperfect and contradictory and beset with divisions, while also offering fertile grounds for hope. Describing a walk along Offa's Dyke in *Footsore on the Frontier*, Jenkins writes:

Borders, frontiers, shadow lines of one kind or another are a familiar and sometimes painful condition of Welsh life. But a walk down the Dyke concentrates the mind on what has made us one, a nation, in spite of our notorious internal dissensions.

Jenkins campaigned for Welsh devolution and international solidarity with the same sense of purpose as he campaigned against nuclear power, militarism and racism. A politically- and culturally-committed poet – *engagé*, would have been the word, had he been a French writer – he was unafraid to be satirical, or epic, or polemical, or to be simply and frankly angry. Auden's (already ironic) line 'Poetry makes nothing happen' did not convince Jenkins, because poetry for him *is* the happening. Words and actions were not opposites, they were complementary: faced with a choice between doing something for a cause and writing a poem about it, Jenkins chose both. A spell in prison for protesting against the presence of American bombers on Welsh soil, and the frequent opprobrium of reactionaries and political time-servers in letters pages of the newspapers (which he relished), attest to that. 'An Execrably Tasteless Farewell to Viscount No', his send-off for George Thomas, the anti-Welsh, anti-devolution and anti-European Labour Lord and long-time speaker of the House of Commons, ensured poetry made the front pages of the London newspapers. Savage and witty, the poem channels anger into craft, reminding us that poetry has often been a thorn in the side of authority. 'Poets are particularly dangerous enemies', reflected *The Observer* at the time.

*

Acts of Union, subtitled *Selected Poems 1974-1989*, appeared in 1990. The title alludes to the acts of union by which Wales was annexed to England, but the book's original cover – a naked couple intimately entwined – suggests that other kinds of acts of union are also part of poetry's purview. The political and the personal are never far apart. This *Selected Poems* takes its cue from Jenkins by starting from *Acts of Union*, and is presented chronologically, up to and including a selection from his last book of poems, *O for a gun* (2007).

Once I had made my selection, I was struck by how the book begins with a handful of poems set on the Gower farm and ends with a series of haiku, and a sequence entitled 'Advice to a Young Poet'. The 'young poet' in question may be any one of the hundreds of students in creative writing Nigel Jenkins taught and mentored across his career, first at Trinity College Carmarthen, and then at the University of Swansea. The 'young poet' may also be his younger self, addressed across the decades, with an energy undimmed by experience. As for the haiku, of which Jenkins produced two volumes, we may think of these as three-line portholes onto other cultures and eras, and into other ways of apprehending the world. A comment in *Blue*, his first book of haiku (published in 2002), gives us a telling insight into the connectiveness of Jenkins's vision:

> An early expression, in Welsh art, of the spirit of haiku, it seems to me, comes not in words but in paint: Thomas Jones, Pencerrig [...] may not have heard of haiku, but his exquisite little study (16cm by 11cm) of 'A Wall in Naples', so at odds with the picturesque floridities of his time, pays revolutionary and haiku-like attention to the numinous life of 'nothing more than' a battered old wall and some rags of washing hung out to dry.

Jenkins compares the haiku with the *englyn*, forging a Welsh link with a Japanese form, and with his own 'Cosmic Gnomes' (included here), based on the ancient Celtic inscriptions known as Ogham Stones. Then, in an inspired observation on the way artistic affinity works across cultures, he brings in Thomas Jones's great small canvas, reminding us that – before it is poetry, before it is painting, before it is music – art is a way of seeing and feeling that enlarges experience. Jenkins's work is about these connections, these affinities and enlargements: Wales and the world, the visual and the verbal, the individual and the community, the present and the past.

This book contains love poems and poems of desire, lyric poems and public poems for public spaces, occasional poems that transcend their occasions, merciless satires, and poems that borrow epic voices, whether of bravado or lament, and retool them for today's challenges. There are poems written in the spirit of high-intellectual play and urgent poems about environmental degradation, militarism, nuclear folly, imperialism and capitalism. There is beauty and precision, outrage and indignation, savage wit and deep empathy. What Jenkins's poetry entirely lacks is hopelessness, and where there is cynicism, it is reserved for those who deserve it: philistines, defeatists and political cronies. The book also contains a number of Jenkins's translations from the Welsh – a reflection of his commitment to the bilingualism and biculturalism of his country, and to the idea of a community of poets.

A sense of history underpins Nigel Jenkins's writing, but it is the present that propels it. In that sense, his poetry and prose are part of a single, albeit various, *oeuvre*. They are the work of a writer who believed that poetry has a duty to engage with the world as it is, while holding out the imaginative possibilities of what it can be.

Patrick McGuinness

FROM

Acts of Union
(1990)

The Ridger

Capsized, by some nosing cow,
in the headland where last unhitched,
it raises to the solitudes
guide-arm, wing and wheel.

What should slide or spin
locks to the touch; a bolt-head
flakes like mud-slate at the push
of a thumb – fit for the scrapyard
or, prettified with roses, some
suburban lawn. Yet there persist,
in a tuck away from the weather,
pinheads of blue original paint.

To describe is to listen, to enter
into detail with this ground
and this ground's labour; to take
and offer outward continuing fruit.

My palm smoothes the imperfect chill
of rusted iron … I weigh against
the free arm, easing up
the underside share – worms retire,
lice waggle away: it stands
on righted beam, rags of root-lace
draped from the delivered haft.

Maker and middleman emblazon
two cracked plaques: Ransomes, Ipswich;
White Bros., Pontardulais.
Less patent is the deeper tale
that gathers with the touch of rain
on the spike which was a handle,
the nail bent over for an axle-pin.

First Calving

Up through the rain I'd driven her, taut
hocks out-sharing a streak of the caul,
and that single hoof, pale as lard,
poked out beneath her tail.

In shelter,
across the yard from me now,
her rump's whiteness fretted the dark.
I watched there the obscure passage
of men's hands and, exiled in crass
daylight, waited –
                      till a shout
sent me running big with purpose
to the stable for a halter.

They flipped to me the rope's end, its
webbing they noosed around the hoof:
we leaned there, two of us, lending weight
to each contraction; the other fumbled
for the drowning muzzle, the absent leg,
      said he'd heard that over Betws way
         some farmer'd done this with a tractor –
            pulled the calf to bits and killed the cow.

Again she pushed, and to first air
we brought the nostrils free; next the head
and blockaging shoulders, then out
he flopped, lay there like some bones pudding
steaming with life.

                  Later,
she cleansed. I grubbed a hole in the earth
and carried the afterbirth out
on a shovel: to be weighted with a stone,
they said, to keep it from the scavengers.

Pig-Killing Day

I watched from the bedroom, all sound
from out there jammed by the music
that boomed inside.
                Then up
from the beech-tops the rooks
unfurled, hung streaming
through dull white sky,
      till a peace below
             drew them filtering back,
and someone turned down the broadcast.

They dragged her from the trailer
like some damaged drunk, his
nakedness snarled with red string,
and in the outhouse where
we'd stewed her spuds, they
hooked her up, paunch taut
for the knife's first nagging.

Heads above bowls
crossed the yard
            all day
as they scraped and scalded,
hacked and subtracted, slowly
spreading the room with pig.

The kitchen by evening was plump
with faggots and strange other
pieces.
         All that remained
of the pig I'd known lay uncurled
in the coal hod, brightened with dust.
They said me goodnight, with their
clean hands brushed me ...

We ate well of the pig, she
lasted us months
                        though for days
I preferred to ride on the tractor, shy
of the trailer, the death
    it brought home.

Castration

Cutting, they called it –
but for all
his noise there was no
blood, no visible hurt:

just some thing in him
halted, to change
a bull-calf to a steer.

It didn't hurt, they said
as they caught and threw them,
locked each scrotum
for a second
in the cutter's iron gums.

The next one was mine:
round the yard we
chased him, brought him
down – hooves flying –
in a slither of dung.

They sat him upright,
like a man for barbering,
and I felt
in the warmth of his purse
for the tubes.
They gave me the tongs
and with all the steel
of my arms I
squeezed them home.

They fetched me another,
said he hadn't felt a thing.
But I wouldn't play.
With all that sky-wide bawling –
    sound his throat

was never made for –
some nerve in me was severed.
There were words about
that weren't to be trusted.

Thrashing Day

A string at each knee as a bar against
vermin, the men piked the rick
sheaf by sheaf to the thrasher's mouth.

To us the mice were Germans
in the farm's gold, or if we came
in holsters and hats, pink infidel
Injun's squirming right for the boot
in their blind nests.
                We'd flick them
half crushed to the cats below,
heroic under the arms of men
sweeping wheat through grey skies.

Hoisted to fame by the legends spun
over midday's ham, we swilled our tea
and returned to the breathless hulk.

A spanner, a few words; the clack
and whirr, belts building the pulse:
we were not to go near, though they gave me
a fork for the afternoon.
The first was a she-mouse pinned
by the spine to our cobbled yard, writhing,
a pinch of life uneasily killed.

Someone shouted as we walked away
through the chaff-swirl and the noise,
but we didn't want to talk.

At seven they put two farmers to bed.

In the dark we spoke of the day.
I thought that in our next game I might
be the Indians – my brother did too:
the world was crawling with cowboys.

Stud

They fancy you from New South Wales
to Kansas, wherever the cymric mane
deranges an horizon. Sun smashes
over that pampered hide, arched within
a bridle's bare control, as you shrug
the bit to be at the mare. Joy-kicks
rent with farts disrupt the clockwork stride
which spirits you – addict, professional –
to where those back legs, dropped for ease
in a tractor rut, are scuffing the earth.

Reins tight beneath her chin – her fidget
arrested by some fear of what her blood
has always known – she stares back towards you,
her juice beginning to bead in the dust.
Your muzzle bumps the place, you sniff
again to prompt the signalling screech,
the raised hoof's proposal of a fight.
Your scream curdles, you rush on, forelegs
hoop her round. Jaw viced on her withers,
eyes rivetting space, you bore into sleekness.

As industries once harnessed you, so
now you tunnel beauty's fiscal mine.
The mare bunches into your thrust; all
of sound and silence warp to this apex.
Two, three, six times daily, quickening to
the jar of flood … And you drop
from her, just able to stand, as day-sounds
prick the tension. Hurried breaths platter
the grass, then it's back to the gloom,
another pedigree satisfied.

Chain Harrows

Diesel taints the sweet stench
of grass and scabbed manure.
Steel's rush, permitting only
tink of stone, drags hanks of couch

from stale pasture: they loll
in the crosswind, a whispered hay.
Third gear work, this; enigma
to Gower's newer eyes, peering

from the roads at little more than
some kind of lawn effect.
The bed reversed for cleaner ground,
I speed in top, dung shrapnel

sketting the air. Glancing back
to keep aligned, I catch
within the harrows' dance a frenzy
of bone – the skeleton burst

of rabbit or lamb. Shards litter
a region of bruised grass
like the spray of feathers
where a fox has killed.

St. Govan's Chapel

I remember it now – that lookout
on the head, the surprise geometry,
half-way down the limestone cliff,
of chapel roof and bell-stock – .
came here as a boy, too fussed
with a kite or a shrimping net
to trouble much over legend lost
to a man-size absence in the rock.

From behind, three jets explode
on the sky, gag the morning's heart
in a blisterous roar, diminishing
over the channel; but it takes
my shadow's memorandum
to flick a lizard-thought-lichen
from its basking stone, down
to trustier depths of shade.

Cofen or Cobhan? Govan or Gawaine?
Your name and what you fled from,
the plea from terror that opened up
stone, fast wither from us.
                           To stoop
inside, I reach for the arch-stone's
finger-digged nook, reading scratched
on the roof-slate some Tony's 'woz ere',
which will be, till next we have rain.

In this clefted apse, here, Govan,
you left your mark; were you man
or woman, the impressed rock chimes
with the stations of bone: scapula,
dorsum, the skull's bland cup. Yet
the lips of your life-grave, kissed smooth
by the scores trying darkness for size,
keep closely the rock's remembrance.

11

Outside, a girl is posing – propped
by the wall: her smile breaks open
the shutter, she slots into prospect.
How well, Govan, you slipped the thing
that drove at your heels. I look out
now on the bay's printed swell,
and your hole is in me: with words
I fumble both hollow and heart.

Cathedral Cave

Nylon and the wisecrack defend us
from the cold; lights a/ and d/c
guarantee the path ahead, machined
through an untidiness of stone.

Cathedral Cave, now gently wet
where once had shoved the waters
of millenia. Moistures collect, fall
to bland pools, the stalactites lengthen –
an inch every ten hundred years.

Ogof yr Eglwys Gadeiriol, fancied
godhouse of a god both got up and
dropped before his maker's voices
first were emptied here, and words
accoutred a numberless gloom
with nave and dome, with organ
and spook organist.

Yet, as we shamble to, guilty with awe
in the great dome, our guide asks are we
scared of the dark, and asks again.
'Can I switch out the lights?' We blink
on a blackness original to stone,
make lodestar the scent of a girl's hair,
a man's loud laughter – till a torch
plucks back each smile from the dark.

In so given a sanctum
nights out of mind ago,
how might the old cavers, the breed
of Lascaux, have delved in sign.
For us – Bach crackling through a timid amp,
and no chance in hell that a single word
could call the roof down on our heads.

Where poems came from

They came, I supposed, from London.
Or from somewhere in England – Heaven,
most likely: wasn't God, after all, a bit
chalky – the grey suit and silver hair,
the underwear somewhat neglectful –
wasn't he the sort, in his spare time,
      to be spinning out rhymes
      on the prettiness of things?

Journeys they claimed –
      over hills and vales,
      through moonlit doors,
      down the last furlong
from Ghent to Aix –
      but they reached us
too heavy for words with chalk-dust.
They were chalk-dust and the tired eye,
they were trembling knees when all went
speechless at the eager end of Friday.
They were paper and they were
      words, books of them
yellowed in the classroom cupboard –
the place that poems truly came from.

Yet truly they came,
behind my back they talked
to me, though I heard no words,
their coming was not to do
with words.
      It was in the laughter of dogs
      way across the snow. I could smell it
      in freshly painted rooms, taste it warmer
      in the cream than the milk. In the tricks
      that skies played with stone I found it,
      I found it in my body when first

I discovered its emptying joy
and wanted, afraid, to share it.

They came too in forgotten
things, in the thing wholly strange –
                    that I recognised.
And one mart-day they came,
in farmer's voice as he sat
drinking tea,
        explaining to himself, trying
        to explain the world to himself.

But not in the words of his explanation,
not from the names did they come.
        For there's a space
        in things, a gap between
        the words for it and a wave's
        movement, its infinite motion.
As I stood,
        a baby, at the sea's edge
        I began to wail – for no misery,
        no joy that I could name –
        lost, quite lost for words

to be facing there our world's great noise,
    to be facing there its silence.

Yr Iaith

She who has forgotten
remembers as if yesterday
the scythe they left rusting
in the arms of an apple,
the final bang of the door
on those sheep-bitten hills.

In Abertawe, in Swansea
there were killings to be made,
and they politely made theirs.

She spent a lifetime loving
the taste of white bread, a lifetime
forgetting the loser's brown.
And on their middle floors
the brass gleamed, the crystal sang,
while away in the attic
dust fingered
the violins and the harp,
and far below stairs a discreet
and calloused tongue complained.

Years she remembers
of cuff-link and shoeshine,
but nothing, she says, nothing
of those dung-filled yards.

It's autumn now, an evening
that ends in colour TV
and the washing of dishes.
I ask her, as I dry,
Beth yw 'spoon' yn Gymraeg?
Llwy, she says, *llwy, dw i'n credu,*
and she bites into an apple
that tastes like home.

Maidenhair

The fern was all I wanted there;
the richer pickings – her lustre jugs,
the family dresser – were spoil I left
for other tastes. Grandpa's fern,
that dwelt with her, dwells now
with me, a mist of light
on the dark shelf.

Have I the touch, the
whispered skills, to bring it
after so hard a season
to its old brilliance?

I breathe *fern*, and say ancient,
link with primal trees
and the forests of heat locked up
in coal. I say *grandpa's fern*

and she who taught me
the naming of this and many things
opens a door
to rooms of sunlight and polish and fruit.
There sometimes we've found him, clouded
in smoke, a froth of ale beading
on his walrus moustache,
as he fumes against
progress, the workers and his gout.

They are dead, and their story.
There were things
I'd meant to ask: when to cut back?
What if, say, something –
a bullet perhaps – were to smash
its jar ... how then to
re-pot – with leafmould or peat?

The maidenhair endures in the Celtic west.
Theirs they kept whole lifetimes
in the same narrow pot.
I'll give it space, learn its ways; help it
flourish, reproduce, watch me go.

The Watch

To pass the time, time after
time in those last long days
he'd take his watch to pieces
and dreamily
shove it together again.

Time passed. And with time's
passing – a lightening
of the load, as one by one
the little screws wandered,
the gems hid their light
in the folds of his chair,
and the glass smashed.

Time passed, and now the watch
is mine. From time to time
it turns up in a drawer,
and I hold it in my hands, cloud
its mirrors with my breath.

His toil remains: the tobacco,
hayseeds, sand of his pockets
gathered round the rim; the hands
of the watch ripped clean away.

And what time does it tell
with its blank face? You can
sometimes shake it into brief life,
and the time it tells is
always never, always never,
never never, always never,
always never, always never,
always always now.

Land of Song
i.m. 1/iii/79

Oggy! Oggy! Oggy!
This is the music
of the Welsh machine
programmed – Oggy! – to sing
non-stop, and to think only
that it thinks it thinks
when it thinks in fact nothing.

Sing on, machine, sing
in your gents-only bar –
you need budge not an inch
to vanquish the foe,
to ravish again
the whore of your dreams,
to walk songful and proud
through the oggy oggy toyland
of Oggy Oggy Og.

Sing with the blinding *hwyl*
of it all: you are programmed
to sing: England expects –
my hen laid a haddock
and all that stuff.

Ar hyd y nos, ar hyd
y dydd – the songs, the songs,
the hymns and bloody arias
that churn from its mouth
like puked-up S.A. –
and not a word meant
not a word understood
by the Welsh machine.

Oggy! Oggy! Oggy!
shame dressed as pride.
The thing's all mouth,
needs a generous boot
up its oggy oggy arse
before we're all of us sung
into oggy oggy silence.

Note with Bluebells
for Delyth

Endymion non-scriptus: a sea,
as they say, a carpet etc.
No:
the bluebells, they
surprise the place, an otherblue
no bunching can possess.

Non-scriptus, blue spoken
green, of ramsons' breath
and rain:
will
fade when taken, speak too much
of walls, the littled world of two.

No still lives!
I kiss yous as you fly.

It's only in motion
my hands breathe your skin.
Stilled,
they grasp nothing but a width of
alone.

To not nor from: only in motion!
With my tongue and all moveable parts
I kiss yous,
kiss you as you fly.

Warhead

I
So too with the sea:
the need to fuss

over rock and island,
gulls, bathers, shipping, sand

to speak
of the unspeakable.

II
And not so too:

the sea has been home,
life swims there still.

III
After such insult

where would the sea go,
would there still be flies?

IV
The first sound allowed me
as the jets head away

is the click of scissors,
Delyth in the bathroom
trimming her nails.

The second
is the wind

piecing together
a shattered world.

V
There is hunger too
in the fatted world,

people starved
of history,
starved of language
and a place to be.

If hunger is all
that some people think
they will ever have

they will not want to save it.

VI
To be now at war
with megalies, amnesia:
the only poem.

Why then when I wake
is it thought of her
more than all this –

the long thinking
of brown deep eyes,
those long-boned fingers,
years, atlantic leagues from me now –

that launches first strike
on the physical heart?

VII

They'll say, the fatted ones,
they just don't want to know.

Death is the embarrassment.

VIII

From a droplet of water
to winds abroad
in curious freedom

there'd be no more friends.

IX

Disagreeable the deaths,
regrettable the damage...

The names lie,
the lies name:

our words commit our suicide.

X

Un-
thinkable?

Nagasaki,
the second thought,
continues to unthink us.

XI

Suddenly this spring
a thousand questions I need to ask
of a blade of grass.

I note once daily, sometimes twice,
the shrill of the siren
at Kittle quarry: 30 seconds precisely,
then, following the bump
of the blast (heard only if
the wind is right),
three short wails, and all
is clear.

It's another of those familiar things
noticed now anew

and I wish that it were not.

XII

What to do with this fear?
Hold it fast, pass it on.

We change now or die.

Snowdrops

I know what I am doing here,

come every year
in the iron first month

to seek them out.

I choose my time, a
day to freeze
the waters of the eye, and
I move through it

– primal caver delving in sign –

to link with light
of the living blood.

*

Last year too soon,

not a white word
in all the wood's deadness.

Home then speechless

to wait.

*

Sky grey and lowering
curtains the wood:

no money, no food: hush
of alone here, cold
of hunger,

last place of warmth

a hole in the head
that's known, I remember, as mouth.

*

A man in a coat
hunting flowers.

Sudden scatty cackle –
the waving of a branch:
a magpie, I trust, has left the tree.

Here, now
the blue gift amazing of
kingfisher flight

would not be believed.
I ask only

snowdrops,
a warmer world.

*

A warmer world?

*

And here they nod
in the cold and quiet.

*In Bolivia the soldiers
broke glass on the ground.
They made the naked children
lie flat on the glass,
they made the mothers walk
on the children's backs.*

Here snowdrops nod
in the quiet and cold.

If the bomb fell on Swansea,
fifty miles away in Cardiff
eyeballs would melt ...

Can
          a flower?
Can
          the poem?

*

Brother dead in Paviland:

the first I pick
I pick in celebration

of the species that stayed
when all others fled
the coming of the cold,

species now trembling
through a darker season of
its own manufacture.

*

Feet gone dead, hand around the stems
some borrowed thing, a clamp
of frozen meat

but

tlws yr eira

blodyn yr eira

cloch maban

eirlys

lili wen fach

– a song in my fist.

*

The owl is with her
the day's length,
and she is sick
of the moon:

her winters are long.

I hand her snowdrops:
she grasps the primrose.

*

Inside from the cold
they boast no bouquet,

just green breath
of the earth's first things.

I find them a glass,
and on the worktable
scattered with papers
I place them

It is enough.

*

Thin sun creeps
upon the afternoon

and the water warms,
bubbles sprout
on the earthpale stems.

They'll die early, yes,
and drop no seed:

the year may live.

Never Forget Your Welsh

I

& not the lingo

bland bitter brewed with Wales in mind
mad March hares even the gogs
2 to 1 against

April Fools' Day
white dragon
lifts the cup to our lips
drink to remember drink
Eurofizz
fond farmers fond miners avuncular ghosts

the *Daily Mail*
owns my
brain

Fe godwn ni eto yes but we
need more than
magic

'sweet snare of yellow mead'

II

bad eggs
tomatoes
articulate guitars

it is
good
to have
friends

it is
necessary
to have enemies

'of the three hundred only one returned'

Keith Joseph you're mad we
hate you

III
fifteen thousand
golden handshake
'for a year over mead great was their purpose'

we live
spectator lives
old bopa Max the white man's Welshman
wet eyes
wet nappies
drinks with Scarlets to
fascist apartheid

say it with baby grand
English theatrical space invaders
greedy halfers pushing for fame

museum
mausoleum

liquid plash of camera shutter

Roddy fucks royal in Bahamas
another first for Wales

IV

guten Morgen bonjour at
Hotel International
bore da what language is that
some of the happiest years of Petula Clark's life
were spent in Wales

land fit for
CB radio
hick schlitz twits
dressed to kill as Yankee GIs
get drunk and screw
londonised droner disco duck spins
Yoko Ono
not too bad for a woman of 50

they
Country & Western
in Welsh too

'and after the revelling there was silence'

finalising light
USA genocide stations

V

Radio One is Swansea Sound
Jason meets Tracy in
glory estates'
amnesia bid

'and in their short lives were drunk on mead'

but
paid â phoeni
Wynford Vaughan Thomas
by appointment to

the sheep of Wales
will keep the people's memory
clean

arise
Sir Neddy Seagoon
arise Gerald Murphy
two years inside for getting caught
then HTV
scrubs the prison soup
from his chin

the people can't
read
history's a lovespoon
or the Duke of Beaufort's
class collaborationist
Banwen
miners'
foxhunt

they want to destroy us

VI
West Glam Welshes on Mumbles
replica individualists
anglo Langland perfumed hawks most
debonair and parlez vous
spraying a little
culture about
the beaux beaux arts so beaux for the soul
no objection to the language but

vultures of unthink
Thatcher their queen
came to the Patti and
told us

go
Maggie Maggie Maggie
Charles and Di
orgasmic grovel
glee-faced serfs no
tongue like a Taff's
for lavish licking of the royal arse

homo erectus
victim of magic
lonely thoughtful in bingo queue

200,000 & rising
'those fiery men from a land of wine'

every day the Tories
check it for bombs

from The Triads

The three abiding ends of a bard:
> peace,
> praise
> & revolution.

I

There are given three names
to this our remnant
of the Isle of Britain, of
Honey Isle, the Sea-girt Green:
Cymru she is called
by those who share bread
in her first & last tongue;
Wales she is called
by those who share bread
in her second that was first
the invader's tongue;
& England is she called
by certain Taffs abroad
who share no bread
& wish for us nothing
but stranger-ness & silence.

II

The three famous bombers
born to this our remnant
of the Isle of Britain:
Williams the Espresso
who in winkle-pickers went
with a bomb to Tryweryn;
John Jenkins of MAC
who gelified in '69
the English royal publicity stunt;
& Heseltine the Mad

from whose ambitions
Westland delivered us.

III
The three punitive changes of heart
of this our remnant
of the Isle of Britain:
the bards' refusal after all
to praise on its birthday
the apartheid-boosting National Museum;
the miners' refusal after all
to stage any gala
in Tory-gone Cardiff;
& Swansea's refusal after all
to donkey-vote for Labour in '76,
the year of Murphy the Bent.

IV
The three pestilential English visitations
on this our remnant
of the Isle of Britain:
Sellafield soup in the Celtic Sea,
of seas the most radiant;
acid Mercian rain;
& government by Tories,
the enemy without.

V
The three benevolent crimes
of the Cambrian bards:
the refusal by Waldo
to pay any tax to the Warfare State;
Pennar's blocking,
with Ned the Bald & Mered the Melodic,
of Pencarreg's transmission of

Bringlish TV;
& the public urination
of Tripp the Tragic
that in the middle of Bute Street
saved from cremation
the burning leg of Finch the Concrete.

VI

The three negative decisions
of this our remnant
of the Isle of Britain:
the vote against Europe of '79;
the vote against Wales of '79;
& the vote against reason of '79
that spread for the stilettos
of the enemy without
a Tory-blue carpet
from Ynys Môn to Gwent.
These the decisions of *Blwyddyn y Pla*
shut factories, mines & the mouths of poets,
faced Wales with her unWelshing.

VII

The three disappearances
of this our remnant
of the Isle of Britain:
the village of Capel Celyn;
the person of Westacott the Wanted;
& the socialism of Kinnock the Pink.

VIII

There are three employments
for England's Glory
in this our remnant
of the Isle of Britain:
warming up the Union Jack;
heating wintry second homes;
& flaring off the flatulence
of Labour politicians.

IX

The three primary arsonists
of this our remnant
of the Isle of Britain:
Saunders Lewis,
Lewis Valentine
& D. J. Williams
who went in soggy homburgs
to the bombing school dumped
by the English on Llŷn,
& struck from words the deed.
Their matches were damp,
but the fire still burns.

X

The three apartheid-caressing institutions
of this our remnant
of the Isle of Britain:
the Welsh Rugby Union;
the Llangollen Eisteddfod;
& the National Museum
whose blandishments were
punished by the twenty-five bards.

XI

The three liquid wonders
of this our remnant
of the Isle of Britain:
Buckley's Best, gusty as the blood
of Carmarthenshire foxes;
Brains SA, the cosmic urban
Skull Attack;
& Felinfoel Double Dragon,
brewed at last
to transcendent perfection
by Cheesewright the Sais,
one of the three most beneficial
White Settlers who ever came
to this thirsty remnant
of the Isle of Britain.

XII

The three liquid abominations
of this our remnant
of the Isle of Britain:
Truman's Triple Crown, a passing imitation
of fizzy cardboard;
Whitbread 'Welsh', a yellowish dampness
conferred on us, England's little butties,
on April Fool's Day, '79;
& Allbright the Vile, which, vets agree,
proves the horse at Welsh Brewers
near the end of its days.

XIII

The three nocturnal moccasin-wearers
of this harassed remnant
of the Isle of Britain:
Siôn Hebenw, whose words on a wall –
'Maggi been here' – are all that's left

41

of Duport Steel, Llanelli;
Dai Hebenw, whose words on Ferry bridge –
'Caesar hasn't a clue what's going on' –
were snuffed by Caesar's secret police;
& Siân Hebenw, who has written on rock
'Guy Fawkes was right'.

XIV

The three obligatory masochisms
of this our remnant
of the Isle of Britain:
paying £1 on the English side,
to cross the Severn;
reading *llais y Sais* the *Western Mail*;
& voting Labour
to keep the Tory out.

XV

The three watery extortions
of this our remnant
of the Isle of Britain:
the price that's paid
to cross Welsh water;
the price that's paid
to drink Welsh water;
& the price that's paid
to pass Welsh water
in the form, already passed,
of Allbright the Vile.

XVI

The three truncated tourist attractions
of this our remnant
of the Isle of Britain:
half a blue swing-bridge;

a titivated forechunk
of the Mumbles train;
& the shattered lav
of Neddy Seagoon.
All, no doubt, what the tourist expects
of a nation itself
only half hearted.

Wild Cherry

Tiptoe on wall-top, head in
clouds of white blossom, I
reached for the fullest, the
flounciest sprays, I travelled
many miles to give you them.

You placed them, smiling,
in a jar on your table,
& there was beauty between us,
between us too were words,
white clouds of words…

One of the sprays I'd kept myself,
& I'll know on what morning
you brush up the petals, you
toss out the twigs with the ashes
& empties, yesterday's news.

To Ms. Evans, with thanks

we'd been both out walking

me in the poisoned mud
of Swansea Bay
& you where no insecticides, the
bouldered headland
of Dewi Sant.

slurried flats at tide-fall, dis-
graced mussels
the turnstones turning stones when
madreperla! I
find, am found by
this cup of slippery light
that here I give you

a shone translucence
no words can tender.

early morning there you picked for me
        bluebells
        campions
        sea-pinks
        ox-eyes
        one guilty cowslip
        'from the hundreds, the thousands'

& there out west
– your dash for the train –
the bunch got left, locked
all weekend
in an office in Milford.

I give,
        you name
your giving:

though I'll never see them
exchange is made
& of no possession
I am in receipt

your wild flowers
        their dawn.

Libya & Child
19.iv.86

Sight this week of the child, first
sonal peep at the moonfish waving,
scratching nose
                  inside her...

& this week wide eyefuls
of the Mad Dog State
mad-dogging the mad dog...

I bike into town. Is this all we can do,
this straggle of 60 harangued at in the rain
by the lightless ranters of the London left
& Maggie-Maggie-Maggied through
streets of wiser anger
than our own squibbish rage...?

At the Con Club chief shouter
whips his drones into a spit, the gob flipped
berserk by a break-siege old Tory
come forth to have us know
– *Maggie! Maggie! Maggie!* –
that he was in the war
– *Socialist Worker! Mad Dog Reagan!* –
so that scruffs like us could march up here
& hurl insults at his club.

I cycle back home, find even the goldfish
– nose to nose where I left them – unmoved
in the murk of their acid-rain pond.

The child goes on reaching
for name in the world...

FROM

Ambush
(1998)

I

(Please fill in name, weight and height)

I, ..., a tensioned heap
of water, calcium, organic compounds,
weighing .... stone
and standing, for now, ... feet tall

blink out from the boneroom
at what little of the all,
and seem, as I stare,
less than a
less than a photon of starshine.

I, like you, am atom matter
born of stars dead, remassed and re-
shattered, through aeons flung
to lodge awhile in a sun's, the Sun's realm
as iron for blood, calcium for teeth,

every molecule of my DNA
as plenous with atoms as the galaxy with stars.

My boot, to be sure, is death to the worm,
I am fifty million million cells.
Yet, like an atom, I am all but void:
switch off my electricity
and – dis-charged the repulsions that bind me –
I crumble to a fine invisible dust.
Like an atom, like you, like a galaxy
I am almost wholly empty space,

vessel and witness of the vastitudes.

The Cosmic Gnomes

1.
Fossilized light; nothing disappears
Though all is rearranged.
Lost are they who are unamazed.

Tân mwyn-ddoe; ni diflanna dim
Er ailosodir oll.
Y sawl heb sêl, sydd ar goll.

2.
Blasted light; stardust are we, luxivores –
The cosmos conscious grown:
Primed for voyage outward home.

Tân ffrwyd-wyllt; lwch sêr, ym hil derwyn
Ymwybodol-cosmos-bryf,
Yn barod, allfyned, adref.

3.
Pulsing light; supernovae tune the Earth;
Atoms dance, atoms sing.
They kill, die who seek to cling.

Tân cur calon; supernovae'n tiwnio'r Tir;
Dawns atomau, cân atomau;
A laddo, ei grafanc, angau.

4.

Onward light; a quasar's gleam, aeons dead,
A face's in a glass:
We gaze always on the past.

Rhagddo dân; lleu cwasar, aeonau crin,
Wyneb yn y drych sy'n rhoi:
In drem fythol ar ein doe.

5.

Dizzying light; more suns than the billions
Whom we starve as we feast.
If all gave, all would receive.

Tân rhoi pendro; heuliau mwy na'r myrdd
A lwgwn wrth in wledda.
O roi dogn, pob un a rodia.

6.

Milk light; we slay the whale yet outsight crave,
Intelligence returned.
Mind's self-survival mind yearns.

Tân maeth-laeth; lladd morfil, encilio'r awch
Adennill ein deall:
Cof goroesi, cof y call.

7.
Measured light; atoms, star-built, grown to know
Space in us, we in space.
Cosmos observed, cosmos changed

Mesuredig dân; atomau, ystum sêr, diwygio dysg
Gofod ynom, ninnau mewn gofod.
O nodi'r cosmos, newidia'r hanfod.

8.
Finalizing light; an eye to the stars,
A foot in primal slime.
We change * con\sider * or die.

Tân y terfyn; trem ar y sêr,
Troi ein traed mewn llaid.
Gwella * pwylla * neu marw sy raid.

Welsh versions by Menna Elfyn

Atom I

! and all, for all a numberless age,
was heat's whole and lightless light

until, radiant, the oneness cooled
and night's inventors, the atoms, danced

dreaming stars and dreaming
the eyes to see them.

Atom II

Indivisible?
Take an apple, take a knife,
slice the fruit in two,
halve and halve again
until, times ninety, you approach

the irreducible:

a little know-how, a
steady hand, and – Hiroshima! –
the at

                     -

              om
                     's yours.

We'll dig iron on the asteroids, mine
awe in the electron.
We particle, we thing,
we jerk into name
the halves of nothing, makers still
of mere history;

unloved the wave, the flesh
unpleasured.

The Creation

When God clocked off from work one day,
   Having put the finishing touches to Wales,
The Archangel Gabriel begged the Creator
   To divest His opus of some of its veils.

'She's the finest,' said God, 'of all my creations,
   A land of quite extraordinary charms,
From her alpine peaks and salmon-packed streams
   To her golden coast with its prosperous farms.

'Her people I have blessed with laverbread and cockles
   Cwrw Felinfoel and great mineral wealth,
They'll be wizards of rugby, singers and bards,
   And they'll speak the language of heaven itself.'

'But haven't you, Boss,' the Archangel demurred,
   'Haven't you somewhat overpaid 'em?'
'Not,' replied God with a devilish smirk,
   'Not if you look at the neighbours I've made 'em.'

Suddenly

Grey mid March her bikeride home;
daily the heave against wind's denial,
the drowning daily of seabird and wave
by the drone relentless rush-time cars.

What then raised her eye
– zigzag skewed in the bundling grey –
was a fiery squiggle of sun-struck cloud.

And that cloud, she knew, that cloud that moment
could change, in ways, a person's life,
could change, once observed, the universe.

Last Word

She, like the planet, lovely and hurt
by squalorous man, shocked the fiesta.
'Why not?' she smiled, congested with grief,
'why not just nuke the whole disaster,
let nature start again… ?
It would be like having a good shit.'

But, they reasoned, there might not be time
for a wiser model to fumble from the wreck
before the Sun, swollen
to a red giant, and devouring its children,
gobbled up the Earth.

'Well,' she said, 'perhaps we should all
self-obliterate, leave the planet in peace
to the birds, the gorillas, the wiser whale.'

A noble abdication, but no, they said, it is
now too late: our machines, our systems –
we cannot simply walk away from them,
there'd be anarchy, melt-down, a thousand
Chernobyls, death world-wide to bird and beast:

we have made ourselves indispensable.

Hello?

This is Neighbour One to Planet Earth –
are you receiving? We are indeed moved
by the lonely hope of your Voyager bid
insisting outward the loving simplicities
of your far from unsophisticated minds.
And to be sure – Bach, Leonardo,
Chekhov, Miles Davis, Dafydd ap Gwilym –
we are not unimpressed. We sense, however,
a reserve, a hesitation – do you receive us? –
about what you might call the crocodile within…

No, the craft itself has not yet arrived –
the fastest thing you have ever launched
won't snail our way for millenia yet, no –
we read your schemes on the radio waves:
in five or six hours, at the speed of light,
tonight's TV will zoom past your envoy and its
lumbering PR to deliver in bits and babel pieces
an other tale: how some Daz and *Dallas*,
how some crawl in the desert covered in flies,
how the happy families scream and smoulder,
snap and crackle, while ceaseless the heat
for the whitest shirt, the sexiest drink –
unanimity only when all transmitters
cut the coffee and chocs to warn of war…

The show so far? Chaotic yes, but vital too,
with a certain primitive originality – Mozart, Picasso –
that is not entirely devoid of interest.
Your knowledge, though, gallops beyond
your wisdom – we speak from ancient experience,
survivors ourselves of the techno-moment.
You are at a familiar turning point,
but don't expect us, who learned at last
to live with ourselves, to drop in and sort you out.

We adhere strictly to non-interference
in all internal planetary affairs,
and we fear that even a courtesy call
could tilt you into panics of self-destruction.

Do you, Earth, do you receive us?
No? Stay tuned, and endeavour to practise your own PR
We'll try again in an aeon or two.

299,792.5 Kilometres a Second

Light leaves us as it leaves the stars:
I see you as you were
a fraction of a fraction of a second ago,
sunned at the window, this bitter day,
by a light that's eight minutes out from home.
We kick heels waiting

for a sudden upturn, the happy accident
while gazing perpetually out on the past:
a quasar as it was twelve billion years back;
a face across the room
whose light hit the road
a hundred millionth of a second ago.

I think us back some years, you and I…
Where now, I wonder, is the light of that time?

The Ballad of Cwm Tryweryn

Cofiwch Dryweryn, the slogans cry
   From walls all over Wales:
Remember, then, for tomorrow's sake
   This most infamous of tales.

Three days before Christmas '55
   The Scousers delivered their gift:
They wanted the Cwm for a reservoir –
   The natives would have to shift.

[Chorus:]
So dam Wales, dam Wales for England,
   The Taffs may not like it much,
But they're snug in the pocket of the British State,
   And a lucrative soft touch.

The multitudes of Liverpool,
   Her Corporation lied,
Were desperate for water –
   Their thirst could not be denied.

Some sheep-bitten acres of soggy land,
   A failing peasant or two
Could not be allowed to stand in the way
   Of progress (and revenue).

Yes, the tricksy Sais omitted to say,
   Though Wales soon caught wind of it,
That their plans had nothing to do with thirst
   And all to do with profit.

[Chorus:]
So dam Wales, dam Wales for England,
   The Taffies won't like it much,
But they're the first to fall to Bringlish rule
   And a lucrative soft touch.

At the heart of Cwm Tryweryn lay
  The village of Capel Celyn
Where Welsh was the tongue that greeted you
  In every single dwelling.

Famed were they throughout the land
  For their poetry and song.
They kept the faith and ploughed their fields,
  And helped each other along.

'Flood Tryweryn?' they gasped at the news,
  'A barbarous, nightmare scheme... '
But the sight of surveyors unrolling their maps
  Was no figment of a dream.

They turned for help to their local MP
  And other Labour grandees,
But with Labour the lords of Liverpool,
  Plaid Bradwyr were deaf to their pleas.

'Do not drown our homes,' they begged
  On a demo through that great city.
Howls and curses, flying gobbets of spit
  Were the measure of Liverpool's pity.

[Chorus:]
So dam Wales, dam Wales for England,
  The Taffs may not like it much,
But with boundless faith in London control,
  They're a Parliamentary soft touch.

Democracy will take its course,
  The restless Taffs were assured:
Tryweryn's fate would be ordained
  By five (unelected) lords.

They set in Wales not a lordly hoof
  In deciding for Liverpool's Bill.

The path was now clear for England's MPs
　　To gather round for the kill.

At last but too late the whole of Wales
　　Awoke with anger bristling
(Except for George Thomas, Eirene White
　　And the usual True Brit quislings).

From Pembrokeshire to Point of Ayr
　　The refusal was full-throated,
But outnumbered as ever, our futile MPs
　　Were – democratically – outvoted.

As the engines of destruction loomed
　　Great meetings in Cardiff were held
Of councils, churches, parties, people –
　　A congress unparalleled.

In vain they called for a scaling down,
　　In vain they petitioned the Queen –
For what England desires England shall have,
　　Brit imperial routine.

[Chorus:]
So dam Wales, dam Wales for England,
　　The Taffs may not like it much,
But they're all for Elizabeth, Charles and Di,
　　And a royalist soft touch.

Five years it took to build the dam
　　And destroy the farms and village.
Not even the civilized violence of MAC
　　Could put a stop to the pillage.

As MAC hit Tarmac's plant with its bombs
　　(To Plaid Cymru's pacific groans),
Tarmac blitzed every building in sight,
　　And heaped the dam high with their stones.

Not a wall, not a tree did they leave in place
      Lest memories should linger;
They even evicted the dead from their graves
      That no bone should point a finger.

As the river rose and flooded the cwm
      Despair swamped the living departed,
And many a bungalowed, jobless refugee
      Died early, broken hearted.

Never again, the Cymry swore,
      Never again such shame...
But mad roads, dead jobs, the scourge of opencast:
      The rape goes on much the same.

And will go on until we find
      In our long unquiet deeps
The road that will lead us out again
      From the dark where our freedom sleeps.

[Chorus:]
Until then it's dam Wales for England,
      The Taffs may not like it much,
But they're snug in the pocket of the British State,
      And a trouble-free soft touch.

Byzantium in Arfon

This too is no country,
at least on Saturday nights,
for old men
or a 46-year-old from Swansea
with a group of (thank god not English) students.
The young in one another's mouths,
gulls machined from the ramparts by
the blitzpop blasting from disco-bars,
the vomit-falls, the can-kicked crowded streets,
fist, yell, or yowl, commend the whole night long
whatever is youthful, loud and Welsh.

'This,' says Zach, 'is madder than Manhattan!'
As well, Zach, you're not some Mercian Mike –
they'd have you bundled into faggots
and scoffed with mushy peas
quicker than you could squawk Segontium.

This conquerors' first, most counter-Welsh of towns, this
Constantinople of the western vertex
where Rome ends and the Raj begins
is by now the Welshmost town in Wales,
exulting anew in the ancient iron
and arcane discriminations.
In the Black Boy a jilted bonker
whines at his mount as she leaves with someone else.
'Look,' she shouts back, *'Rwy'n i ffycio fo heno*
a chdi y-ffycyn-fory.'

Caught in that nasal music all neglect
the dazed Yank, the inadequate *Hwntw*...

If, come Sunday, I bid their walls
a glad enough farewell
it's not to say I won't need to return
to their hard fold, this necessary north
where empires come
and empires, *diolch i'r Cofis,* go.

Abergwaun '97
for Ozi Osmond

Had Jemima and co. been less Brit and more Cymric
   Et un petit peu plus frolicky,
We'd be living today in a red wine republic,
   Not a moribund weak beer monarchy.

In/dependence

any fish can fly

in the belly of a gull

Fanfare I

let trumpets unleash

from forgetment's cave

the practical dream

Fanfare II

that all in green song

in all courses move

Capital
after Ionesco

the Welsh for London is

Cardiff

Postcard

Came for a day:

setlo am oes ...

By Other Means

i.m. Epynt, Capel Celyn, Selar, etc.

In times gone by they ripped us off
    By the might and main of war,
But nowadays they help themselves
    Through the trickery of law.

Four Translations from the Welsh of Menna Elfyn

1. Kids' Play
to Siân ap Gwynfor and all who occupied Carmarthen
District Council's nuclear bunker

'Kids' play!'
            the jibe, a
hoarse first-strike
at the motley band come to
squat beneath the scaffolds,
late summer drizzle snaking down
the blue fertilizer bags
that shield us from the gawpers.

Doll's house play:
a stone for a table,
a rock for a bed;
a roof we can reach through
to gather wild flowers…

'Peace' is the die that's cast in this game.

*

Fields, out above Cwrt y Cadno,
like grease-paper spread
over iced *teisen lap*;
you two ready, a tobogan apiece,
ready for the slope, to go sliding crescendo
                        downalong
                                down
                                    on those
rails a-screech like some new breed of bird,
each sledge unrolling
                        a new-knitted scarf.
'Give it a go!'
            comes the call –
me scared of a slithery bruise-up,

but the urge, of a sudden,
for knowledge's sake, to go
                              go
go rolling, ground zero, in a white explosion
                              like a snowdrop,
a snow-bell,
three snow-gems in the dust.

Yes, that's how it was, our day of
snowflakes, day full-tilt of
                              whooping
                                        freedom.

*

Through today's cynic brays
thoughts surface
of then and that snow: of kids' play
before they stumble on the stone of 'commonsense' –
                              play safer, it would seem,
than these bitter games,
                              the games of grown-ups.

2. Shoes
in a museum of Resistance and Nazi memorabilia

Way-worn by Oslo
one Sunday afternoon
our feet sought out
a museum's gentler pace:
a museum of shoes,
regiments and regiments
in row on neat row
of children's shoes,
removed and set down in an orderly manner
before the little ones were gassed of an afternoon.

So bereft of meaning are shoes without feet.

Stout little shoes,
shoes with laces tied and hardly worn –
unsplashed through puddles,
unscuffed against bark,
not a toecap to bewail a fall,
no leather creased into durable smiles
by the deft percussion of tiny soles;
shoes hinting of
just-beginning-to-walk.

And that's how
there erupted this blister –
through bearing witness
one Sunday afternoon
to a people and the manner
they met their end
so noiselessly
in their stockinged feet.

3. Love's Scales

The night's pursuit of her
was nothing to the moon,
then his dark highness
flung down all his weight in a heap,
human granules,
and, lifting up a fistful of dust,
dunked a finger in to taste their blackness,
sucked of them along the dark's scales,
pressed them fearfully together, a dowry
craving warmth – and there was
no resisting night's impulsion,

the weighing and the measuring,
the releasing, decreasing, lowering, considering –
the steel scale's ancient way
of diversifying mortals, as it hurls them together
in love or in pain, gram upon gram, their flesh dissolving
on a dish above the stars' too tender chains.

The weighing, the measuring, there's no holding back the night,
our instincts too frail to deny its sortings;
the dark enfolds us, limbs quake,
the kilos huddle tight until dawn divides.

4. Raincoat in Asheville

Leave home without a coat?
Not on your life –
even jaunting through a land
where a cloak would seem uncalled for
the damps of my nation
will find and drench me.

No one else was flashing a mac
or brandishing brollies,
yet the gentler the weather
the more we've reason, in our thin weeds
to fear its sting.

How timid, I declared at the bar,
how unventuresome the Welsh
'No one would dare leave a raincoat behind
for fear of a deluge –
still less neglect a *negligée*.
We like to keep dry, swaddled against
all outbreaks of flesh.'

I wonder if I could
undress my tribe,
flay them naked of every last stitch
and leave them dancing in the rain,
puddle-struck adventurers
levitating through a champagne monsoon.

But as a matter of dampish fact
I was caught myself
holding in Asheville's neighbourly summer
both court and coat,
black coat that in the heat
of a bluegrass moment

got left, a nylon heap, on the back of a seat.
Yes, I of the tribe of Don't-Get-Caught
was caught out with a vengeance
– 'A fair rain behind her' –
as I landed back in Wales,
a girl empty-handed
praying for a storm.

An Aside from the Dunghill
'The Prince of Darkness is a gentleman...'
King Lear III.iv.147

Walk on: obey: walk off
why trouble the great tragedy
with a death like mine –
shrugged out on the dunghill,
run through from behind when I
upped and said no
to the murdering of his eyes?
The old man himself,
weeping blood at both sockets,
they flung from his hearth
to smell and fumble
his way to the coast.

Servant 1, Servant 2 ...
Nameless men like me
are not men but shadows
and the bearers of shadow,
casting lengths of a lord
wherever he commands,
fed or beaten as our lord is liked,
the shadows of machine.
How could I have stopped them?
Better to have kept my nerve
for the job
than to end like this, my own eyeballs
pressed wide with dead pain
in the castle's shit.

But how it rattled their cosmos
when the silence I was bred for,
the yes-my-lord-no
cracked under weight
of that old man's scream.

From the womb I'd said nothing,
less the pattern of patience
than scared as beaten dogflesh
of hunger's maddening road.
They bred me to serve, to carry the cup
for their ceremony of words
and to wait, without ears,
as their large speeches
wriggled land through the banks
and eased to an early grave
lives no longer of use to the plan.
And I
did my job. I watched from the wall
as unkindness fattened
and banished plain love,
as daughterly words
grabbed a father's kingdom
and stripped from his head
the last leaf of patience.
I have seen feelingly
age punished, pity robbed,
justice to its popping eyeballs
in gold.

And I was one
of the gang sent to fetch him.
We shoved him to the room
where his guests were waiting,
and there we bound up
his corky old arms, there we
lashed him
for their hail of questions,
for my lady to tweak out
a hair from his beard.
And there it was,
against all the conventions,
that my lord himself
skewered from its socket
the scream that stripped me, that
drove me between them, thrill'd with remorse,
to prohibit their game.

It was she that stopped me,
she that stuck me from spine to belly,
shutting my upstart noise
from the scene – for her lord,
though mortally knived by me,
to jerk away
the old man's last eye.

I begin now to rot
in the strata of dung,
forgotten by the great and
bourgeois critics,
the gleeful despairers.
The curtain's down,
down and yet
I trouble the play,
voice whispers from here
that if mine were the hands,
hands under fear that
bound the old father
and viced him into pain,
mine are also the hands
that with flax and with eggwhite
laid salves on the outcast's
bleeding face;
that if ours have been the hands
obedient for lifesblood
to a dog in office
ours too are the hands
that obey nothing,
when the jackboot strides,
but the voice it crushes.

I rot into dung,
and there is good,
if you can use it,
spread upon the land.

Meet Me Yesterday

O the lives we live without hardly our knowing...
I had called to you, smothered in quicksand,
and you were too busy with flying
to come, I had thought myself obliterated
by the fabulous flapping of new-found wings.

Then into this morning of accountancy and rain
there came your letter and its invitation
to a life in your life
I'd not known I'd been living:
meet me yesterday, you said:
time, you'll know it; place, a little bistro
not far from the Thames. And you welcomed me in
to your yesterday
with coffee and *very groovy* jazz,
and there I lingered, my breath you said was in you,
my eyes you could feel ensorcelling you.

And look, you said, inviting the alleged
love of your life to clamber (it was getting intimate)
right inside your brain
and compose there with you a seasonal haiku:
'As I drew on my roll-up, the wind breathed a sigh
through the last of the – '
when who should drop by,
for decorum's and orchestration's sake,
but Pablo and Raymond and the sisters Roche...

It was some party, yet not so sweetly loud
that I couldn't decipher
your heart's acrobatic, contradictory news.

But if, now and then, you can find me yesterday
where I thought I had no business to be,
what, I wonder, are we up to today,
and where, o wayward, might you take me tomorrow?

Rendezvous

And we are not the same:

our bodies since then have
one and a half times
changed their cells:

this version of mine
has never known
that version of yours.

Teetotalitarian Lament

'Pour, oh pour that booze away,'
   Said my conscience when it came to call
And spotted the dozen bottles of hooch
   I had laid up in the hall.

So I pulled the cork from bottle one
   And poured it down the sink –
Apart from just one glass of the stuff,
   A little farewell drink.

Then I pulled the cork from bottle two
   And did more or less the same,
Except this time I drank two small glasses,
   For which thirst must take the blame.

From bottle three, three glasses I took,
   From four, yes, four I drank.
Then I grabbed hold of both the bottles
   And poured 'em down the sank.

I pulled out the cork from sink number five,
   Poured the bottle down the glass and drank it,
I then pulled the sink from the cork of the next,
   Bottled seven whole pours and sank it.

From the next full sink I pulled the glass
   And bottled the cork down the pour,
I pulled the cork from my throat, the glass from the pull,
   And drank a few sinks more.

When I had emptied everything
   I steadied the house with one hand.
And counted with the other the bottles and the corks –
   Some fifty at first I scanned.

I counted again when the houses came by,
    And got 'em all, about a hundred, I think –
All except for one house and a bottle
    Which I promptly proceeded to drink.

The Gallo-Saxon Muse

I am a Wales-based writer,
    The English call me Welsh,
So, bless him, does my publisher
    (Not, note, *Anglo*-Welsh).

I was born, it's true, in Purley
    To a taxman and his wife,
But my ex-hubby's step-great-grandma
    Lived in Chepstow all her life.

I moved from Hove to deepest Cowbridge
    About a year ago;
Now I'm as Welsh as Kingsley Amis,
    Princess Di or Geoffrey Howe.

But I am not parochial,
    From all jingo I am free:
I write about universals –
    My garden, my cats and me.

We postmodern Wales-based writers have
    Some civilising to do
In this land of bards retarded by
    Penguin's *Hanes Cymru*.

What use is all this history,
    All these fusty, bardic arts –
Save that I seem by their reflection
    Exotic in foreign parts?

'Foreign', of course, meaning England
    Where I'd never have made the grade
Unless I'd upped sticks, dug deep for some roots
    And resurfaced, hey presto, Welsh-made.

So glide aboard the Taffy-train,
    Become a Wales-based writer:
Wales and Welsh writing belong to us,
    The future couldn't look brighter.

Porth Cwyfan
for Roland Mathias

Cold June for me too, snouting round Aberffraw's fields
    for the lost *llys*, the rubbled
    steel that only once since then
– when all of a wonder, there, long sought, this other is,
the island parish riding aground in its *comfortless bay*,
    your froth-tormented lines made flesh.

Old Marcher bard, old no-nonsense
bridger of the crazings and shoulderer wide of rust-tight doors,
    take for your own
this pre-Cambrian chunk of sea-rolled gneiss, who wound me
    by welcome, by words unblinding
    back to the lost elementals.

I found it in a pool, as green in water as an eye or hope,
    as I stumped the mashed causeway
    to that bell-bereft
        ark of stone,
no dog to yap me, but, nipping still at respite's heels,
    the British fact, Gwynedd be damned,
of those Hawks training, for sales and votes, to murder
    a far-away nation's soul.
What more than this impotence can we call our own,
our peninsula's bedrock by plague and stormwreak weathered down
till we are islands to each other and dead to the world?

I stumble where you strode – choosing, seeking – the lost rockway
    from isle to isle, a bee among us.
If I know Roger Parry, fogged beneath lichen by the north wall,
    it is thanks alone to your witness,
the unrhetorised song you beamed throughout the greendays' froth
of Luxembourg, horse shows, patchouli, grass,
    the conformities of rebellion.

It has been a work, this journey, a revolt in affirmation
        of the beseiged particularities.
        Can I name what I find
on this deck of matted couch and wind, that has and has not
sails of dunlin, *pibyddion y mawn*, shrilling their lone
        to the far planets?
There's a cargo here of more than bones,
though the door you walked in through, and Llywelyn and them all,
        is locked to me.

It was all to me once, as still to most, a phantasmagorical dust,
having neither language nor yet the language
        to find in glum stone
the lubricious, scintillant life it can sing.
This dried chunk I send you of ancientmost Wales,
this monolith *maquette*, I raise to you now
        in the imagination,
where it stands, rain or dry, an enduring, oceanic green.

A Length of Rusted Chain
for Tony Conran

They sang in Welsh their Saxon Reservoir: Llŷn Celyn would speak
– let by-gones be gone – not a word of English,
would breathe not a gable, not a drowned branch
to excessively stir the memory's silts...
        a lake,
        a lake in Wales,
        a Welsh lake...
the anglers their fish, the poets, the painters their English views
and generous compensatory terms, the full mod con.

I give you, Tony, breathlessly late for your festival,
this chain plucked, in the year of heat and literature,
from the sun-crazed silt of Cwm Tryweryn,
and call, south to north, *in the iron of our chains*,
on the lightning that glints when rocks bomb in the boiling *Twrch*
        to fire this hand,
      to boulder down all the rivers of Wales
a restorative rage, a dam-dementing intelligence.

There are chains and there are chains. Yours of gold unites,
twines back to the *warm belonging root of us*, and sings us on.
This too unites, from Venta Silurum to Holyhead,
      link by rusted, impotent link.

    Ddys cwd bî ôl ddat wî haf lefft.

Gone, for blind profit, the stealthy copse and holy quilted fields,
gone harp and hymn,
gone the sanity of walls, the ruminant boulders,
gone bridge and drunken moon,
gone *cymhortha* and *cynghanedd*,
gone bro Tryweryn, the untranslatable, non-re-locatable life,
gone even the dead, their carcases evicted
that not a bone embarrass this murderous simplicity.

We are good at water: rivers, lakes, the dripping tap of elegy.
　　　Beauticians of defeat, failure junkies,
　　　we *cwtsh* at last into 'never again',
　　　for Plaid Bradwyr vote ever again –
　　　　　　　and it's
Cofiwch Dryweryn, Cofiwch Selar, Cofiwch Olew Aberdaugleddau.

One golden day that Indian summer
I stumbled down from the fast new road to walk along the old,
and my eyes were not dry, I could find in my heart
not a sliver of postmodern irony to defend me from the history
that – rubbled, dynamited, scorched to the stump –
had lain for parched months wide to the sky:
the skeletal walls bereft of pasture; the streams gouging mud
to find again the stone of their beds;
a slate, a spoon; and here, whole, Celyn's bridge
bridging again a resurgent Tryweryn…
And at Hafod Fadog, in a room of air, a secret room,
I found creatures ungrasslike of silt and dew, found
where harrows had sung good heart to the field
　　　this crippled torc.

　　　Rattle it, shake it, send its cracked peal
to the malls and brasserias where the liberators doze.
Come, you deconstructivist smilers, come you requirers
that Celyn like Cymru never is, was nor ever shall be.
Come and stand on the grassed and Tarmaced heap of it all,
　　　feel beneath your feet
the very stones of the houses, the chapel, the school
that seasoned the packed rock of Cymru's damnation.

About the Yangtze dams' uprooted millions
　　　we deserve no say
who do not hear, for the jet-skis' narcotic whine,
our own lost – of *Efyrnwy, Clywedog, Cantre'r Gwaelod*…
　　　Felly, Cofiwch Dryweryn!
– and cofiwch too the carcase-worrier's sweet inertia…

Consuriwr, mentor, poet of our country's future tense,
may this chain I send you translate in transit
    from a thing of enslavement
    to the links that learn us unity
and like you remember, sing like you, remember tomorrow.

The Residue

Carboniferous limestone, oil:
the collective memory...

We nibble at light,
forge from stars dead and a living star
the cells that invite us
to linger awhile
as they die, repeat, die, repeat...

Though we lose in a life
– buried in carpets,
sewered to the sea –
ten more or less material selves,
the singularities persist:
rough face and name,
guiding loves, precise guilt...
persist and leap each body's leaving.

Unrepeated, unrepeatable
from here to before and after all...
then smoke, ash,
when? blue sky, blue sky, who?

Vanished tricks of dust and light

tapping like snowflakes
at the 'lids of the living.

An Execrably Tasteless Farewell to Viscount No

The Viscount of No, Wales rejoice, is dead.
White man's Taff
And blathersome stooge of the first 'Order!'
Orgasmic in ermine,
May his garters garrotte him.

O Death! For past misdeeds I almost forgive you
Now that you've lightened our land of this load,
The Lord of Lickspit,
The grovelsome brown-snout and smiley shyster
Whose quisling wiles were the shame of Wales.

Queen-*cwtshing*, BritNat, *Cymro Da*,
The higher he climbed the acider the rain
He pissed on his people
As he stuffed them with Prince shit
And cheered as the voice of Tryweryn was drowned.

Now he's a No-vote,
His goody-buckled-two-shoes dancing aflame
In his Hell of our Yes.
The hand that crossed that paper –
All power to its arm.

Fuck me to heaven in a bath of champagne,
The rending and gnashing of the Viscount's No,
His old 'Order! Order!' 's sweet disorder
Is youth to my ears,
It's a cowin' glee-bomb.

Some Words for English Viceroys, Rugby Players and Others, in Abuser-Friendly English, To Help Them Con Televiewers That They Can Sing the Welsh National Anthem.

My hen laid a haddock, one hand oiled a flea,
Glad farts and centurions threw dogs in the sea.
I could stew a hare here and brandish Dan's flan,
Don's ruddy bog's blocked up with sand.
Dad! Dad! Why don't you oil Auntie Glad?
Can't whores appear in beer bottle pies?
O butter the hens as they fly!

FROM

Blue
(2002)

frosty bark

    as I squint the Pleiades

of fox, cadno, fox, fox

from the pub sways

a choir, tied and suited,

on a cloud of aftershave

    she introduces

her baby to his shadow:

he waves, it waves back

above the pines

Bonny Tyler's palace

outshines the moon

against sunned red brick

the pink white explosion

of a lone cherry –

and I don't want to leave it,

the pavement, the day, this tree

she turns on long legs

away from the bar: not as

beautiful as feared

sweeping the cliffside's

exuberant gorse

a kestrel's shade

I see it —

the palm blooming

just down the street

— first with my nose

first bloom on my back

of this year's newly warm

newly hostile sun

as we breathe out,

scurrying through the park,

the trees breathe in

                                        smacking lushly ashore

                                        from the bay long becalmed –

                                        the vanished ferry's wake

shirt thrown to compost

to be eaten as earlies

in a year of two

sheet of newsprint

leaps beneath a car's wheels

– comes out dancing

the bunched daffs drool

as she grasps with both hands

her ninetieth spring

horse jerks from grazing –

without seeing you

I see you coming

not just any perfume

but hers, months later,

on a passing stranger

scored for piano –

it goes with me through the world

my daughter's music

from this moonless length

of blackest wall

is born,

suddenly, a

girl in a coat

for me, alone,

the shooting star shed

by her pink begonia …

as, busy about the kitchen,

she kisses my neck

FROM

Hotel Gwales
(2006)

Handbook

From anti-void to supernovae,
from the mating of matter
to the rebirth of seas
and the invention of gods,

it has come down to this,
this callus grown
on a fleeting finger
from the daily struggle

to unearth, perhaps, a word or two.

*

If the hand has written everything,
every thing has written the hand.

*

Alone or cupped together
– for nuts, blackberries, water, sand –
you reinvent, daily,
the first bowl,

and could spill, no doubt,
a bean or two
pertaining to the second,

a slice of blood-tight cranium.

*

And then the thumb,
cruising above the prairies of the palm
and docking tip-to-tip with
one finger after another,
achieved fecund opposition,

sparking speech, circles,
straight and sometimes bloody lines.

*

Though you've come a long way, hands,
from those invocatory savannas
you have not forgotten

the padding of palms
upon waterless earth,

or a notion, among trees,
of fruit that might not be

unreachable

*

Branch, stick;
         stick, club:
handy how
– with the grip you achieved
as you climbed those trees –
you invented killing,

though aeons would pass
before you came

to discover death.

*

You built nests, gathered fruit,
scratched the head as you fumbled,
fumbled for stooped millennia
at those exclusive hides,

until you were minded
to breed from two stones
the blade that set you striding
through valleys of meat,

on your way, with scalpel,
to the brain.

*

Striking stone, you struck fire,
striking fire, you struck the voice
that called hand unto hand

to bring meat to its knees

and to articulate,
even of tundra,
a homely country.

*

Knapping stone,
felling mammoth,
plucking leaves,
piking roach,
scraping skins,
cupping berries,
sewing hides,
dragging wood,
fretting fire,
spitting meat,

harvesting the time

to start work
on this poem.

*

Hand to mouth,
fruit by fruit,
grain by grain,
the palm always, at last,
lethally empty –

until the idea
of tomorrow took root:

the hand that then put by one seed
had plans – temptatious rhyme – for greed.

*

The arm, a trunk;
the fingers, five branches;

the deeds of those fingers

blown leaves blown
where there's world to see them.

*

Lately this itch, this itch to crawl
far into the deepest deep of a mountain,
to distil there in paint
the wind-winged, essential herds,

this persistent itch, embellishing a spaceship
with patient blueprint of an open hand,
to catapult pictures into the dark.

*

Hand after hand
from dawntime falling
to the bed of clay,

until there come the fingers
– collapsing horizons, eroding the dark –
that carve in tablets of aluminous earth
intelligence that flies
from tomorrow to tomorrow.

What say you, death?
What say you now
to the hand of anon?

*

The escape from gravity:
to be up there in the tree,
dreaming hands into wing-tips;

to be out there in space,
a Voyager cargoed
with multilingual, sempiternal ads

that say much of the fingers,
little of the fist.

*

For each firm-hearted cabbage,
every trove of spuds, he gives
thanks to his hands.

Praise of god he saves
for the useless rose,
celestial handiwork
that brings him already
close to heaven.

*

The fist that kills a fly
(and writes the fly into this poem),
the index licked
for honey or snow,
the nail dark with whose menses –

the public, the private, the secret
lives of hands:
if people and police
knew the half of their tale

it would be
flee-from-me and handcuff time.

*

Through priestly Chaos they reached,
the Mediterranean fingers
of farmers, sailors, shipwrights, weavers,
to fathom the irreducible atom,
opening the eye
to the godless, holy music of Cosmos.

But the hand on the tiller
is lately of half a chaotic mind, proud
that in its pride the in-
divisible has been divided,
and dithering unto omnideath
'twixt fission and fusion,

as Cosmos awaits
                if not us
                        then others.

*

There are special rooms,
rooms for the fist

that are full of questions,
hair and blood,

rooms constructed
by hands never held,

by bodies and lives
uncaressed.

*

The back of my hand:
I know nothing if I don't know
these sinewed and latticed
fourteen square inches, their
sunned hairs as countable as stars.

But there has been this night,
and whose hand is this
that tells no tale
about the scratchmarks
smearing stubbed knuckles –

where even is the star of day?

*

You, who drive in your cars
to gaze at the ocean,
whose blood's chemistry echoes the sea's –

don't you find suggestive
that unemployed web
'twixt finger and thumb?

*

She told me how
a red and smaller-than-a-pinhead
spider, shy at first
of the warmth of her hand, had
climbed up onto
her index finger and
legs a-fizz
– though she'd felt not a thing –
set a knuckle-ward course.
Such then such
the insistent sunlight
boring pink passage
through the nose-flesh of her cat –
but she'd not dared the distraction
for fear of smearing
the scarlet traveller
through the blonde treescape.
So with one mouth-blast she
blew him clear,
though she has long wondered

how and whether he survived
that fall to concrete
of a metre or more.

*

Blessed the hand, desire willing,
that recovers, at night, between parted thighs

a way back to the sea
when love swam with unhated love

and fingers were fins.

*

Souvenirs of cooking and love –
the smell on my fingers
of garlic, of desire's lubricious liqueur…

oases, oceans filling my day.

*

How does it happen, the estranging of hands
that hunted, once, the tablecloths in pairs,
voracious for the touch
that liberates lips and closes eyes,

hands that when parted
would roll between four fingerless palms
the thirst of continents, the hunger of seas?

How does it happen
that these hands that felt their way
to a body's soul
would no more reach for those now

than seek their ease in acid or flame?

*

Nothing bigger, once,
than this fist-crushed can
at the water's edge.

*

We watched and we listened to
the work of his hands: he drugged us
with blues and the blues drugged him

with money, women, narcotic fame

until he and his albatross
seemed at last
to disappear from his life.

His remains, years later, were shown
on TV: a jobless recluse,
with every fingernail grown
a twirling foot long,

that no guitar
would ever again
sneak its way into those claws.

*

Have you noticed how clean,
when he hands you your change,

are the butcher's hands?

*

She is the latest to discover,
in how many more than a million years,
that her hand composes

the perfect cup for her baby's head.

*

An orderly hand takes
a measured shuffle

across the page,
making note, for some reason,

of yon red tower
and the uncle who had
to spend a lifetime there,

a hand disinclined
to blood with burden
of its own ravened nails

the immaculate square.

*

Reopen the wound, that half-inch of white
aslant the thumb's splayed mons,
nothing to be ashamed of, the left's
blood bombing the chemicalized earth,
just a slip of the right, secateurs mis-angled
to snip not a grapestalk but crunchy flesh.

The scar recalls only the best of times
– *vin rouge* by the bucket, agricultural feeds,
the workers rewarded with each others' bodies –
of which the cicada,
secateured neatly, legs thrashing, in two,
is but the least of green and yellow things.

*

These veins tonight, these
lumpy back-roads
snaking the handscape,
how close they press
to murderous airlight,
how easy it would be
to visit them.

*

If I seem sometimes
to have the backs plumbed,

what scant attention
– unsold on hocus-pocus –
have I paid to the palms;
though so much closer to the action,
they seem sometimes another story.

But I've only to look to my dreams to know
that in this hand that has never hit a child

a monster sleeps.

*

My father's hands, in death's labours,
would toil at his brow
as if in the hayfield
his father and his father
were swiping sweat and seeds
from a yawning head.

What turns of hand
are dealt by sperm and ovum?
The killing I want done these days
is work for hired hands,
but would I slit a throat of duck
or the gullet of a Norman
with a familial touch
perhaps borne in the bone
from Cro-Magnon times?

– though younger by aeons
than the hand of all my fathers
that glides home to warm seas
along my lover's thigh.

*

Okay, okay, it's a right-handed world,
and don't we left-out lefties know it?
You've got it made, brother – 'tool of tools' –
from scissors to corkscrews, from nuts and bolts
to the zippers on flies; it's you that gets to open
doors for the ladies and the doors of ladies,
or to work the throbous rise of a cock;
yours the adroit and prestigious jobs
– look at you pushing that poet's pen –
while, sinister and gauche, 'the hand of the privy',
I get the unskilled, twilight chores. But if I can't so much
as peel a spud or sign this scribbler's name,
let me remind you, Mr Right is Might,
that mine is rarely the finger on the trigger.

*

The hand of power was extended
to the hand of power;
for a second or two
their palms united composed
a tiny galaxy awaiting stars –

and two peoples risked something
approaching a smile.

*

The hand on your shoulder
and the silence it keeps –
are you leading
or are you being led?

*

The soldier – as my splayed hand's
little finger and thumb
began to coax your nipple's rise –

the soldier amputee
who could still feel the pain
in his missing hands

would not be absented.

*

Out of touch with the world, straitjacketed
in shoes, we are seen, if seen at all,
as hands manqués, whiffy might-have-beens
whose digits could barely transport a twig,

good for no more than stomping a beat
as the fingers of Hendrix booglerize souls.

O maestro of the shoelace, we are not
such antipodean cousins:
until we stood and walked our ground
you too were a scuttle of thumbs.

Footloosened at last to finger into being
your prestidigitatory realms,
there are things of earth perhaps
you have misremembered –
humility, unison, the receipt of pleasure.

So, come, touch; reach down and touch:
this too – the toes a-splay,
the arching and curling – this too is transport.

*

It has been decided
by the most complicated object
in the known cosmos

that two fists will be made,
one of the left hand, one of the right,
and that these fists will be conjoined

knuckle to knuckle, wrist to wrist,
like two thoughtful hemispheres;

whereupon it has been further provided
that the faintest of smiles
may ghost the lips in celebration

of a simile's homage
to a working relationship

older than the first cupping of rain.

*

Having slept the sleep of white ocarinas,
the baby wakes: in those crystal coals

that no colour yet has dared to name
there is all and none of the world's story,

as old men drift through her
and star-flung dancers, many hands passing by,

fingering space, beginning slowly
to remember themselves.

On Four Paintings of Evan Walters

1. Self-Portrait with Candle

We have two of everything here
– don't we? – two of everything here…
The Artist, capital 'A', at binocular war
with *that dull robot the camera*,
the beret's black halo,
the 'tache of office and tuft imperial
declaring for Art and daring
– with two candles twiced –
to conjure such fire
as to pale the sun's paling
of his right that is not his right cheek.
You'd need a mirror to unmirror him,
to find palette and brush in left hand
while the right, off stage,
works its restless, incendiary magic.
From the revolution they will not buy,
he will not, the eyes insist, be deflected –
not by critics, curators, *Mam o Nedd* herself,
though the robot within
has long concealed a counter plan,
has long concealed a counter plan.

2. Boy with a Feather

it is

it is as if

it is as if
gravity itself

'twixt fingers as if
and lips as if

were in

suspension

3. Rear Admiral Walker-Heneage-Vivian

It comes down, the eye comes down
past ribbons, medals, tassels, stars
and almighty sleeves
to those fingerly bones
and that democratic cigarette –

and then returns
to the eyes at blue sea and the wreckage
of a smile.

The master, Walters, of *HMS Powerful*
has not got all day: there are
pheasants to be shot, communists to quell,
daughters to be avoided, and, above all,
rhododendrons to raise.

If a fag ain't the sum
of the Admiral's joys,
he will draw small delight
from this dauber's lurid dabs
as imperium's peacock cries its last,

though they're the best, if not all,
that will one day remain.

4. The Artist's Mother Asleep

There, he has said it, dared in paint to say
what the sleeping mother's son won't have said.
The son watches for the stertor to wane,

117

a gummy smile to sink that shark-snout head
as he brings her just a half cup of *cawl.*
She breathes, breathes still, who for son and painter
black-leaded the grate, kneaded dough, plucked fowl,
hallowed the language, affirmed the scriptures,
and once, for art – to *drws nesa*'s alarm –
took most of a morning to peg out one sheet.
Though the son has hedged her with orbic charms,
the painter, who has heard the stertor cease,
has created of the bed that bred him
his mother's iron and his own coffin.

Once Upon a Time
for Branwen

Come, as the whitebeam, come Bran again
to the big old bed, and I will
read to you while the silvering wind,
and you, Bran, will read to me,
Dad a page, then Bran a page.
From this 'rock of Harddlech overlooking
the sea' there are ships to be seen,
and in the blue beyond, arrivals of blood –
though may fiction's door preserve
our pillowed heads from tragedy's lethal absolutes.
Can you hear what I can hear
way across the years, those pigeons hallooing
a dawn brazen with the so much still
that was left to come? Do you hear now
this owl of a wind that will bring us soon,
until perhaps again, the last of leaves?
As birth's trumpets forefanfare a death,
so first smiles, first words, first christmases
are invisibly murmurous of the last.
There's no sitting any more on Daddy's knee,
and soon enough, your hand, like your sister's,
will banish mine on the school-pally streets.
So come, Bran, again to the bed that bred you,
we've a book to get read, you take the right page,
I'll take the left, and in the name of all
the Branwens who've been happy
we'll not open yet any Cornwall-facing doors.
The day will come, I know, when you'll
fly without your redundant co-reader,
but for now I am with you in griefless *Gwales*,
ready, when you yawn, to dog-ear a page
until – wait 'n' see – tomorrow maybe.

Forty-Eight and a Half

Here I am, Dad, this is the month
I overtake you. Let's do it on horses,
you on my mother's black-maned mare, me astride
the grand if mildly delinquent bay (whose bones are
where now, whose teeth and tail?). I'm coming up
on the outside, Dad, only a stumble can stop me now,
and no flogging of a corpsed cayuse can keep you ahead.

Foxhunting Taff with a penchant for the shires,
you had your Scotch and Three Nuns, your loud afraid laughter
warmed a place you were public schooled not to understand.
But when nights were nights and seasons knew their place
you made a harnessed pony of our lives, her fulfilled leather
creaking with sunlight, as taut as taut words
in the right abode. Then things went, metaphorically speaking,
all to fuck and boarding school buggery, the dreamplate
departed Mum's hand, missed your head and broke
a family's heart: too much horseflesh, too little love.

There were furlongs between us. To your Brylcreemed mohawk,
the revenge of tresses sufficient to thatch
an army of Guevaras; to the alleged music of Sir Harry Lauder,
the orgasmitudes of Hendrix. I didn't want to be a farmer, Dad.

But, neck and neck, through the months of your heart's
perplexed liberation, we found forgiveness, found in each other
the boy and the man, a stander of rounds
to your interrogative sea-lost eyes.
It wasn't long, dark horse, before you cantered free
on the prairies of night: did my brother not tell you
of the sweet one-nighter who declared him at dawn
nearly as good as his dad inside her?

Night, though, had another plan: the black wart that was not,
to which you took an agricultural knife, sporing
cancer through every field of your liberated land.

It was daylight, scorched-earth robbery.
The Old Pilferer's taking his time with me: the odd
tooth ripped off, half an acre of topmost turf purloined,
and a heart, like yours, in laconic turmoil.

So here I come, Dad, after twenty-seven years
the plashy nostrils of my lathered mount are panting down
your skeletal neck, you'll be lost any second
in flying hoof-scoops of earth and grass – unless, unless,
yes, c'mon, gimme your hand, I gotcha: leap!
Cwtsh up, Dad, *cwtsh* up behind me, we'll ride on together
in galloping tandem, my daughters will sing for you, we'll
raise a few rooks from the beech-tops yet;
so put baccy in your pipe and pass me the Teacher's,
there be horizontal times ahead.

'Is that where they make the clouds, Dad?'

It is beautiful, the filth gusting
from a stack at Baglan, turned by late sun
to a wing of silver
rising against
the blackly green, languorous hills;
beyond the great dapplers bundling east,
an unearthly simplicity of open sky;
here at our feet the tide bangs in,
loud lengths of it slapping
the concrete steps.
There could be rain. There will be night.

An Uncle's Satisfaction

I want, Tom, my twenty pounds,
and spare me, please, the rebound
that, pissed then, you've no recall –
it just ain't believable:
like too much of what you say,
mere smile beguiling wordplay
or hammed affront – as when I
groaned 'Loan? You mean a bye-bye.'
Though twenty quid's no big thing,
it isn't all that's missing.
We want, *gwboi*, to rescue
what's left of you that rings true.

Beautiful still, my *brawd*'s son,
my girls' cousin of cousins –
your life awaits your arrival,
but it can't, Tom, survive all
the glee-gobbed and woozy bane
of this chronic holiday.
Still the party's boy of boys,
you are heartbeat's overjoy,
ear-tucked fag 'neath Burberry,
jiving hot galactic eyes
and unschooled intelligence
reeking, still, of future tense.
You're wanted on the dancefloor,
not shrinking to some bar bore,
the saloon's lord of earbash,
generous with your father's cash,
taxiing from deal to bar,
cadgerdom's fly superstar.

Tom, you're loved and I'm afraid.
The Unreal Arm's barmaid
has a cliché of a plan
for the boys of Neverland.

Sickness, madness, prison, death:
you, before your thirtieth,
could fall through lush vortices
to one, two or more of these –
unless, Tom, an inner tide
can turn against this lifeslide.
Turn, then, those two ready fists
to hands that are harmonists;
that calculating deal-hand
to thought's daring fountainhead;
and that lone heart so self-twined
to a re-peopled turbine.

You won't like this poem, Tom,
that sees into your maelstrom
yet fails in its forensic
to feed you an easy fix.
You alone can help yourself,
not some uncle's bardic bombshell.
I want, yes, satisfaction,
a debt that's paid and not shunned,
proof, Tom, you've not given in:
you owe your life its living.

A Body of Questions

What would seem to be the matter?

*

If our blood distinctly remembers the sea
what vague recollections of supernovae
dwell within our atoms?

*

So these cells got together
and invited you
to make yourself at home?

*

Is there anything more ambitious than a cell?

*

If we all start as women
what is it
that makes me a man?

*

Do we think because we learned to smell?

*

For how long have you inspired the sky?

*

Where precisely have you been
the last six million years?

*

Just looking, eh?

*

Don't you, as you
blink out from the boneroom,

don't you change it all?

*

Do we ever forget – tee tum, tee tum –
the warm symphonies of the womb?

*

Why not be naked and unashamed?

*

Can you feel your chemicals touching each other?

*

If the heart's so full of love
how does it find room for the blood?

*

Who can resist the Islets of Langerhans?

*

How far from the mouths of our caves
do you reckon we've parked our cars?

*

What do they make of all this Space Age food,
our Stone Age stomachs?

*

Is happiness simply the absence of pain?

*

Is hell the pain
we know we cause others?

*

Will the wave be loved, the flesh pleasured?

*

Do you, wet skeleton,
do you play hearts?

*

Have we taken the Earth
and lost the Sky?

*

But listen in your blood
to the song of our sphere:
aren't you too an astronaut?

*

If it weren't for touch
and its addictive delights
where in all Creation would we be?

*

When the heart was set in place
somewhat closer to the loins than the brain
did a smile cross the celestial lips?

*

With so much salt
in our blood, urine, tears, flesh
is it any wonder when lovers kiss
that oceans collide?

*

Fishy, eh?

*

His nine, her ten holes,
the perfect leather coat:
aren't you touched?

*

One of life's little

solitary pleasures, uh?
uh? uh?

*

Don't you feel, enquired the tooth,
that death keeps taking
little bits of you?

*

Is it lonely down there at the big toe,
such a long, cold way from the capital?

*

Is not the harvesting of light
the only work that really matters?

*

Wouldn't you get a better view
of the icebergs of Antarctica
or the lover you've lost
if you closed your eyes?

*

For how much longer,
as we breathe out,
will the trees breathe in?

*

Was not that expression
on your grandson's face
your great-grandfather
taking a walk through him?

*

Is there anything that DNA doesn't know?

*

Is food a matter of time?

*

How many deaths
– spiders, pigs, worms, flies –
have you notched up today?

*

If the cells you're made of
replace themselves every few years

how much younger, do you reckon,
is your body than you?

*

Do you think we've been visited?

*

Can you hear it –
one universe ending, the next beginning:
God's stately heartbeat?

*

Who'd've imagined
that the ear, assailed by molecules of air,
could deliver such open-heart surgery?

*

Whence this addiction,
this ferocious addiction
to the private ownership
of individuals?

*

Doncha find a sneeze out of season
as holy as the tickle
of healing wounds?

*

Is it not a return
to the unhurting dark
from which we came?

*

Would there be, without death, a single poem?

*

Has there ever been
an obligate aerobe
with so many questions?

'A Las Cinco de la Tarde'
or 'Life is not a stroll across a field'

(Pasternak)

for Margot

It was five, exactly five in the afternoon
but I was too foozled with grassy reefer
and summery love to heed the clockwise cry
of yon buzzard prof. of Spanish lit.:
the farmboy would take his city girl
on a stroll across a hilltop field,
its dandelions, its harmless cows.
Seventy or so innocuously nosey
black-n-white droolers snortily circled till I
batted them away
with a whoop and seasoned farmerish wave.
I wuz az high az dem mooz wuz crazy:
my whirligig arms stirring ever faster
a gargantuan cup of Friesian tea.
It was five, yes, five in the afternoon
when professor buzzard, reeling on high,
decided to remind a deafened ear
of the twentieth century's number one word, 'b', 'u', 't' …
And at five o'clock, as the lover and his lass
were most of the way across that field
the bovine circle halted before us
and turned at once
into a straight and panting, asthmatic line,
a cohort of incontinent moos-at-arms
with not so much as a horn between them,
no, not a horn, but, *madre mia*,
through the end of that nose, o what a ring!
and o what a burning in that field marshal's eye
of pristine murder, immaculate rape.
Women and children first, MarGOt!

But is it run or is it walk?
Is it butt or is it gore?
Head sunk at the ready, snorted breaths
stamping the grass, he permitted his playthings
an elephant's lifetime to reach and scale
that gate of barbed exquisite wire.
'I'll be back,' he mooed, 'I'll be
back one day, fences or no… '
One day, butty bull, doubtless you will,
but for now it's steak *au poivre* to you.

Punctuation Poems

;

Semicolon

Cwtsh up, o dread-struck,
to the jinxed, the best avoided,
the point that panics;
I will not, if you come to know me,
dement or destroy you.

I am the point of balance,
a glass of iced water
at the half-way hotel.

It could all end here, yes –
but it doesn't; there's more and maybe
better to come.

Colon

If, these days, I play less than second fiddle
to that single-minded stopper of every show,

I am popular still where appetites
have expectations – the Americans adore me:

I promise and – old stager – I deliver.
I have ambitions for us all; but one for myself –

to bridge my divide and become as one –
is a future it might prove unwise to explore.

,

Comma

Bourgeois, you say?
Managerial, I'd prefer:
everywhere at once,
fit and vigilant,
sorting, dividing, clarifying,

and master of the inspirations.

What happens in the end
is no business of mine:
I'm engaged to ensure
that things proceed –

though in the fog that descends
when lawyers decide
I've got out of hand
I may be the maker of mighty trouble.

Dash

I am – you've noticed – the great
disruptor: there's a violence in me
that can stem – at a stroke –
a river's flow.

Mistake me not
for the frenzied penman's
dash-of-all-trades
nor for my wee, hyphenating cousin.
I may seem, sometimes, a cheery joiner

but disconnection if not erasure's
my line. I have only to unite
– nineteen-forty-nine DASH –
your first date with your last

to write you out.

Though it may please you all
to call me dash,
I am not, if need be,
incapable of patience.

—

Hyphen

Let's be friends, if not lovers.

If wars have blundered
across my bridgework,
so too, in time,
have the treaties had to teeter.

Let the swaggering dash
go loudly about his disruptive game.
I, at half the size,
am the line that combines –

though not for me, fear not,
exclusive matrimonial rights.
I comprehend the atom's
binding repulsions,
the together that remains
a free-breathing twain.

( )

Inverted Commas

A twosome, always,
untouching yet inseparable,
like a marriage gone to speechless seed.

We raise curtains, sound fanfares,
and seal, when all's said, the silences.

We have, ourselves, nothing to say,
one loneliness turned in upon the other,

and mocked by *soixante-neuf*'s mirage.

)

Apostrophe

The unbuttoner, maybe, the *relâchez-vous*.
Get me right, though, before you're seventeen,
or be haunted for life
by cabbage's, potato's, spud's 'n' pear's.

I prow, yes, the absences,
my presence proof,
when I'm found where I belong,

of something missing, something possessed.

• • •

Ellipsis

If you're inclined,
not to notice
the… gusting
from that stack among the pines,

then for you, blithe waltzer,

I am footsteps eternal
in everlasting snow…

!

Exclamation Mark

Sexy! Real! Hilarious! New!
I rear tumescent
from flaccid horizons,
spinmaestro of spectral thrills.

I'm the short cut
to a cul-de-sac
that's painted to look like
the heart's highway.

Don't even think of
loneliness! age! poverty! death!

I

Italics

Look at me. I said *look at me.*
That's more like it.
Where there is weakness, you see,
I swagger into power.

I have only, yearning rightward,
to raise my voice

for all, fore and aft,
to declare their undying
insignificance.

And if, sometimes, I'm obliged
to *SHOUT*, it's then, maybe,
that a little light fascism
comes into play.

Full Stop

Whatever in life
is muddled, side-stepped, misconstrued
there is no ignoring me,
full stop, new sentence.
And should that sentence prove
too painfully long
you have only to invoke
my easeful abbreviatory skills,
full stop, new par.

Whichever way you wind –
via colons of plenty, dashes of joy –
I will oblige you, ready or not,
with your vanishing point.

'£23 will save a life'

So we send forty-six.

We do not send
ninety-two
or a hundred and eighty-four.

We buy the kids an ice cream,
ourselves another bottle of wine.

The Cucumbers of Wolverhampton
from the Welsh of Ifor ap Glyn

I've made this alarming discovery –
it's been like a blow to the ear:
the cucumbers of Wolverhampton
are Welsher than people round here!

It's something I saw in the paper,
I could hardly believe my eyes,
but there it was in black and white –
and *The Sun* don't tell no lies.

I was thumbing around in all innocence
between the racing and the Page Three pets,
when I saw in this piece that our bodies
are nothing but chemistry sets!

Giblets and bones are what's inside me,
I'd believed until that day –
not calcium, potassium,
carbon and water –
even iron, so they say.

True love may well be likened to steel,
but there's iron in every man too;
there's iron in the bosom of every woman,
and silicone in the breasts of a few.

Although we're quite rich in iron,
we're seventy per cent water, or more!
(Though why the water doesn't rust the iron,
the scientists aren't quite sure).

We're all H_2O, a full seventy per cent!
It's a fact you can't gainsay!
Gallons and gallons of Tryweryn am I
as I slosh along my way.

Now, the people of Bilston and Handsworth
may not sound as Welsh as they oughta,
but they drink what flows from Tryweryn
and they're seventy whole per cent water.

So they're Welsh by pipage, if not
parentage; the census is therefore wrong:
a barrel of Welsh red water
is each Leroy, Singh and Wong.

And so in the Midlands of England
there are ten million lost Welsh others;
isn't it time we pushed the border back east
to embrace our abandoned brothers?

It would solve all our problems with tourists:
they'd be living in Cymru too,
with Powys spreading to Norfolk,
and Gwynedd ending at Crewe.

A great *Sun*-reading brotherhood,
sharing alike both friend and foe.
I don't mind being on a par with the Sais
… but second to a vegetable? No!

Because now here comes the downside.
The paper then started to number
the contents of animals, plants and veg –
including the cu-bloody-cumber.

While there's no shortage of water in us,
cucumbers have ninety per cent!
The cucumbers of Wolverhampton
are Welsher than Gwynedd and Gwent.

So if some cheeky blockhead comes along
proclaiming to all in sight
that he's 'more of a Welshman than you',
don't reply 'You looking for a fight?'

Just put on a knowing smile and say,
'That's nothing, stop making a fuss –
the cucumbers of Wolverhampton
are Welsher than every last one of us.'

Airstrip St Athan
from the Welsh of Iorwerth C. Peate

God in his wondrous grace a garden did sow
between sea and mountain, whose paths would ease
the wearied people to meadows whence would flow
the waters of Bethesda, Eglwys Brywys's peace.
Many a cheerful village he sprinkled there –
Llan-faes, Aberddawen, Y Fflemin Melyn –
dazzle-white gems in the grasslands' care,
and hedge, lane and dune with tales beyond telling.
But now they're as dust, all passion broken on the wheel –
unhappy man whose wants he cannot quell
turning leisurely roads into highways of steel
that deliver nothing of Llan-dwf's peace or Llangrallo's spell.
    And the gracious Vale, from 'Barry' to 'Porthcawl',
    is raw meat to greedy hell's mechanic sprawl.

The Shoulder of Lamb
with a nod to William Carlos Williams

so much depends
upon

a Welsh sheep's
shoulder

braised with *rhos
Mair*

beside the white
earlies

Englyns
from the Welsh of Ifor ap Glyn

Englyns are akin to scampi –
no one's sure exactly what they are,
and you're usually sorry you asked…
for anyone who fancies
that he can explain them
is about as engaging
as a talkative bore when you're busting for the bog,
a CSE in biology,
a member of the SDP,
or last week's *TV Times*.

It's in school that many first stumble upon them
… along with bullies,
the whiff, in the chem lab, of stew,
and everyone else's hand in the air
when you don't have the faintest clue.

They don't teach much that's useful
to you
in school
like:
how to unfasten a bra;
but they *do* teach you
such invaluable things as
how to deconstruct an englyn.
What's the use of learning how to strip down
the carburettor
when there's nothing more that you'd adore
than a driving lesson
in an englyn afire on cylinders four!

Englyns are not a kind of bratwurst…
a bratwurst has no trouble raising laughs…
especially if it's a 'stand up' bratwurst.

Englyns can't be compared to dogs.
An englyn will neither give rise to fleas,
nor fetch your new slippers as you take your ease,
it'll simply inform you that the old pair
were so much better than these.

Englyns are also unlike ashtrays;
they can hold things that shine
as well as what's ashen,
and no parlour should be without one
in case a poet should call.

Because englyns are ancient –
A kind of bardic bouncing cheque –
they're like last night's curry, inclined to come back
after fifteen hundred years –
and that can't be bad.

Writing the little devils
is as much as ever a fag,
but things will be somewhat different
when we've englyns that 'boil in the bag'.

Advice to a Young Poet

It is a journey towards the unknown.
Perhaps your only clue is the Saharan dust
that ghosts, at dawn, the paintwork of your car.

There'll be camels en route and kif and jellabahs,
but the place you arrive at
will be quite other than you could have foreseen,

and you too will not be unchanged.

*

It has to do with beginnings,
it has to do powerfully (weak word)
with the rearing force that seeded you,
and with the unimportant, vital shards
that you've plucked from the stubble
and that you will not yield
to the oblivion

about which
it has also to do.

*

Know language, know languages, know
your own language, that you may take words
beyond words: a poetry

of leaps.

*

To serve the poem
you will need to be
in a devotional trance;
cast a spell perhaps
with music or a walk or a stern espresso,
then savour the occasion

of pulling up a chair
to the making table;
savour the paper, savour the pen;
raise a glass, if you like,
– of water, coldest water –
to the planet and this life,
blow the muse a hopeful kiss

and write.

*

May your night be sleepless
until you are at least on speaking terms
with the stranger-word you met today.

*

If you despair
that no word
can do more than fumble
at the reality of a wave,

take heart
from the oceanic force
that churns in the space

between word and word.

*

Words of all kinds
have their uses,
but don't forget the power
of little words – the 'then' twiced
that brings a bitter *hiraeth* home;
the abstracting 'and' that makes such music
of 'a little tiny boy'.

Be sparing, though,
of one small, one-letter word
that's often too big for its own boasts.

*

There are some words
so 'ensorcellingly' (for instance)
full of themselves
that you'd best not use them
more than once
in an entire book

– if not in the whole of a writing life.

*

You will be instructed,
container of multitudes,
to get a voice, just one voice,
and, having got it, to superglue
that priceless commodity
to your bardic being.

Ignore such calls
to monovocal bliss.
Listen, instead, to the wayward voice
of each new poem.

Many poems. Many voices.

*

Avoid the poetic:
the typeface designed by garden gnomes;
the bespoke poesy
of words like 'forlorn', 'myriad', 'russet';
cheap 'n' easy lists of plants and things
with fabulous names;
the routine molestation of innocent nouns
by posses of pervert adjectives;
p p p p p p p p p p p p p p p p p pseudo-
experimental party turns
designed to impress;
sub-Dylanesque word heaps

designed to impress;
sandyfloss confections like
'the parrot of his confusion' and 'the lumbago of her doom';
waffly abstractions lost in space;
rhymes that only rhyme;
lists like this.

Your aim should be
not fog and tricks
but accuracy and magic.

*

Do not expect a slap-on
of numerology, tarot
and recycled hocus-pocus
to conjure up the magic –

it will come, if it comes,
through the arteries of speech.

*

Wait, after the latest
tanker disaster,

before wading in
with an ireful ode

that does nothing but add
to the poetry slick.

*

The tree improvers, who thought themselves
poet, demolished the willow

that graced the entrance
to the graceless building, replacing the tree
with a branchy installation

unloved by all.

There are times when a poet
should do precisely nothing

except let trees speak for themselves.

*

Go for a pint, now and then, with Dr Williams
– or Herr Brecht, Monsieur Rimbaud, Señor Neruda.

until, with his book on your knee
in the rumourous bar,

you get to know him on first-name terms;
he may even, before the night's out,
buy you a pint.

*

Attend, keep note:
you may not remember
in a day's time, let alone a year's,

this morning's red admiral
lowering, after rain, onto steaming slate –

unless you break from kissing
to write it down.

*

Praise, by all means,
the luscious drama of locking tongues,

but honour too the everyday,
and do not neglect your dreams.

*

Though a good critic could save
your poetry's soul, beware resentful destructors
and the scientising jargoneers.

Your adviser too –
he may be semi-toothless and scraggy of pate,
but he too has a frightening amount
still to learn.

*

Don't be cowed by a brush
with anyone's canon.

*

Poems, *au contraire* – and not least in Cymru –
have made many things happen.

Word surgeons, speech architects:
poets are among
the language animal's makers of life.

*

Sing for Wales, sure, but don't shut your trap
on all the rest – it ain't crap.

*

The straight thrust, lethally honed,
may cause, on occasion, creative offence;

but for memorable action,

slantwise is wiser,
as is out from behind
who knows what bushes.

*

Don't spend too much time
drunk/in bed/doped/watching TV/
waiting for the *awen*.

You haven't got long:
only, if you 're lucky,
some 300,000 wakeful hours

– and the art school dance
is already long past.

*

Even in cold, unpromising weather
keep the door at least ajar –
encourage visitation.

Tick over, perhaps,
by transcribing a dream,
baking bread
or translating someone else's lines

until that moment, sooner or later,
of groin-tingling ambush.

*

'The poet must know everything,'
Hugh MacDiarmid forgot to say
that Rilke said.

*

It may sometimes be there,

but here is rarely
too small a place.

*

Know your place – its rocks, its soils,
the movement of its waters –
not only by maps and histories
but by body and residential mind.

Walk it, eat from it, drink its rain,
ask among its breezes

for sign and sound
of those who filled their lungs here
when the mammoth roamed
or when coal was a possibility of trees –

dis-cover your community.

*

Know your place. What legends and myths
have had their shaping here?
What stories, novels, histories?
And who have been denied a voice?

What songs, here,
await their singing?

And how, in this place, worker of the word,
might you make yourself useful?

*

Know your times.

Who's got the food?
Who's got the money?
Who's got the water?
Who wants the oil?
Who's got the bombs?

And as you, lucky winner, flush
your piss away with drinking water,
you might ask yourself
what a poem might need to do
to imagine a tomorrow.

*

It is a music.

*

If you're afraid they'll call it prose
then that is their pedantic problem:
if what you have written
does what you want it to do
(and a little more),
then it's in with a chance –

let it loose

to go about, if it can,
its business in the world.

*

The poem, remember, has consequences,
is a made, additional earthly presence:
what you say (and more) will be what it does –

and lives,
if only in infinitesimal ways,
may never be the same.

*

Don't content yourself
with those clouds skating the water's calm:

be wise to the weeds,
the fish unfathomed.

*

Having come down firmly
in favour of snow,

think instead

coal.

*

Delight, of course,
in the play and shapeshift
of this serious game,

but don't flinch from asking
of your new-born creation

'Who needs it?'

*

Bear in mind, as you write,
that this poem

could be your last.

*

You may have, from the outset,
your creation's last line,

but a poem's ending is not its end.

From

O for a Gun
(2007)

how many of the dead,

as I climb these old stairs,

do I pass coming down?

my shadow at

sunset makes me

ten times the man

not crying

– this girl with hand to bowed head –

but phoning

over the rooftops

a white plastic bag breaks free

from the binmen

high tide, full moon and

fighter jets – if their pilots

could smell this woodsmoke

the slaughterman halts,

opens a door to free himself

of a fly's buzz

the wind returns

– now the leaves are back with us –

in full voice

gull hooked, trailing

from its beak a yard of line –

o for a gun

though she's been gone

for months, they're still a couple

on the answerphone

We do not see

til flight tilts them sunward –

oystercatchers

Iwan Bala is one of Wales's leading artists. Born in north Wales, he spent many years in Cardiff but now resides in the Gwendraeth valley. He has held solo exhibitions annually since 1990, participated in many group exhibitions in Wales and abroad and is represented in public and private collections. His work was exhibited in four Chinese cities in 2009. He has published books and essays on contemporary art in Wales.

Patrick McGuinness is a poet, novelist and critic, and Professor of French and Comparative Literature at St Anne's College, Oxford.

Notes

The Cosmic Gnomes:
These 'gnomic verses', or 'gnomes', in an adapted form of the *englyn penfwr*, were commissioned by Swansea City Council for incision in slate on the walls of the Tower of the Ecliptic astronomical observatory on the seafront. Ultimately, six of the eight (nos. 1, 2, 3, 5, 6 and 8) were selected to appear on slate plaques carved by the Rhydaman calligraphic artist Ieuan Rees.

Although one of the oldest of the Welsh bardic forms, a famous example being the ninth-century lament 'Stafell Cynddylan' (Cynddylan's Hall), it seemed an appropriate model for a commission touching on both cosmological and human affairs. For the early Welsh nature gnomes, which combine the classification of natural phenomena with aphoristic wisdoms, represent perhaps the beginnings of science.

The Welsh gnomic stanza is sometimes compared with a somewhat better known three-liner, the Japanese haiku. Concision, observational accuracy and a strict syllable count are features common to both forms, but they differ in important respects. The more youthful haiku is concerned with particular times and places, and will have nothing to do with proverbial utterances, whereas the gnome is a sententious statement about universals.

Characteristics of the *englyn penfyr* include a syllable count of 10, 6, 7 (sometimes 8) per line, a rhyme between the second and third lines, and, when the *englynion* appear as a chain of stanzas, a continual light touching on a single idea at the beginning of each verse. The first part of a traditional gnome, often the first two lines, is descriptive – usually of nature; it concludes with a line of folk philosophy.

The poet Menna Elfyn who translated my English originals into Welsh has imbued her *gwirebau* with strong and mellifluous elements of *cynghanedd*, the ancient system of sound-chiming within a line of verse.

The figures separating each pair of gnomes are hieroglyphic representations of a planet, the human hand and a star. In Ionia in the Aegean Sea, the birthplace of science 2,500 years ago, the hand was revered as the agent of intellect and the means whereby the Ionians, who were the world's first atomists, could reveal the order ('cosmos') behind the supposed chaos of their universe.

299,792.5 Kilometres a Second:
is the speed of light.

The Ballad of Cwm Tryweryn:
'Cofiwch Dryweryn' means 'Remember Tryweryn'. 'Sais' means 'Englishman'. 'Plaid Bradwyr' means 'the party of traitors'; 'Bradwyr', of course, chimes with 'Llafur', meaning 'Labour'. 'Cymry' means 'the Welsh'.

Byzantium in Arfon:
– with apologies to W.B. Yeats, author of 'Sailing to Byzantium'. Ancient tradition associates Caernarfon, or Segontium, the Romans' most westerly legion post, with the eastern capital of the Roman Empire. Caernarfon's old name, Caer Cystennin (Constantine's Fortress), was also the name used for Constantinople, and Constantine himself was believed to have been born at Segontium. '*Rwy'n i ffycio fo heno/a chdi y-ffycyn-fory*' means 'I'm fuckin' 'im tonight/and you to-fuckin'-morrow!'. '*Diolch i'r Cofis*' means 'Thanks to the people of Caernarfon'.

Abergwaun '97:
Jemima Nicholas (d. 1832), according to the legendary interpretation of 'the Last Invasion of Britain' at Strumble Head near Fishguard, or Abergwaun, in 1797, is supposed to have frightened the republican French into submission with the aid of a crowd of local women.

Fanfare I, Fanfare II:
Both fanfares were commissioned by Swansea City Council for incision in a wall in Singleton Street, Swansea, 1989-1990.

Postcard:
This poem was commissioned in 1996 by the City and County of Swansea Council and the Family Housing Association (Wales) Ltd. for the walls of a new building in Christina Street, Swansea where the second phrase ('setlo ar fyw'n fodlon') differs slightly from the version here, 'setlo am oes', which means 'stayed a lifetime'.

The Gallo-Saxon Muse:
Penguin's *Hanes Cymru* is John Davies's masterful *A History of Wales*, available in Welsh and English.

Porth Cwyfan:
This poem, about the bay in Ynys Môn of Porth Cwyfan and its islanded church of Llangwyfan, refers to a poem of the same title by Roland Mathias. There is a reference in the third verse to the role of RAF Valley in training pilots of the Indonesian air force to fly British-made Hawk jets, which have been used genocidally against the people of occupied East Timor.

A Length of Rusted Chain:
This poem refers to the destruction of Cwm Tryweryn by Liverpool Corporation in the late 1950s and early 1960s (see 'The Ballad of Cwm Tryweryn' on p. 61 for details). The two italicised quotations are from the poetry of Tony Conran.

An Execrably Tasteless Farewell to Viscount No:
Somewhat after the Irish, via Patrick Galvin, of Séan Ó Murchadha na Raithíneach, 1700-62.

Once Upon a Time:
The poem refers to reading the tragic story of 'Branwen ferch Llŷr' in *The Mabinogion*, in which seven warriors, who have returned from the campaign in Ireland, live on the island of Gwales (or Grassholm) off the western coast of Pembrokeshire, without ageing or in any recollection of their former grief or pain – until one of them disobeys an injunction not to open 'the Cornwall-facing door'.

An Uncle's Satisfaction:
The form of this poem is an adaptation of a traditional Welsh poem of request, using aspects of the *cywdd* metre, namely lines of seven syllables, arranged in couplets, the accentuation of whose end-rhymes alternates between the lines' final and penultimate syllables. The Welsh poetic tradition of *Cynghanedd* (lit. 'harmony'), based on complex alliterative patterns and internal rhymes, is described in the *Princeton Encylopedia of Poetry and Poetics* (1993) as 'the most sophisticated system of poetic sound-patterning practised in any poetry in the world'. Very few poets, including this one, have any success replicating its effects in English.

A Body of Questions:
These questions, bereft for the most part of rational answers, resulted from a

commission from the Princess of Wales Hospital, Bridgend for some poems on the theme of the human body, for a glass artwork in the hospital's foyer. Designed by the Swansea glass artist David Pearl, the artwork incorporated versions – some of them translated into Welsh by Menna Elfyn – of about sixteen of these questions.

'A Las Cinco de la Tarde':
'*A Las Cinco de la Tarde*' (at five o'clock in the afternoon) is the percussive and ominous refrain that rings through Federico Garcia Lorca's famous lament for the bullfighter Ignacio Sánchez Mejías.

Advice to a Young Poet:
This sequence is a response, to some extent, to Harri Webb's short – and in some quarters infamous – poem 'Advice to a young poet', which reads in full: 'Sing for Wales or shut your trap / All the rest's a load of crap.' (Meic Stephens (ed.), *Harri Webb: Collected Poems*, Gomer Press, 1995). *Hiraeth* is one of those famously 'untranslatable' Welsh words meaning, roughly, 'longing'. I owe the observation on Shakespeare's song-lyric 'When that I was *and* a little tiny boy' (to be found in both *King Lear* and *Twelfth Night*) to the poet and indispensable critic Tony Conran. *Awen* means Muse.

Acknowledgments

I owe grateful thanks to Angharad Jenkins for her generous help and advice, and for the warmth of her encouragement, and to Branwen and Delyth Jenkins for their support for the book.

Thanks also go to Margot Morgan – for her enthusiasm and support, and for helpful comments on the selection.

I benefited from the advice and encouragement of John Barnie, Daniel Williams, Robert Minhinnick, Menna Elfyn, Gillian Clarke, Tôpher Mills, M. Wynn Thomas and Emily Trahair. I am especially grateful to Iwan Bala for the cover image.

I first met Nigel in 2000, soon after moving to Cardiff. He was, in person, as he was on the page: generous, erudite and fearsomely witty. His friendship was life-affirming and his writing has shaped both my relationship with Wales and the fulfilment that relationship has brought me. My thanks to him are ongoing.

PMcG

PARTHIAN

LIBRARY OF WALES

POETRY 1900-2000: ONE HUNDRED POETS FROM WALES

Edited by Meic Stephens

The most legendary names in poetry from Wales – David Jones, Idris Davies, Vernon Watkins, R. S. Thomas, Dylan Thomas, Dannie Abse, Tony Conran, Lynette Roberts and Alun Lewis – are featured here alongside many living greats such as Gillian Clarke, Pascale Petit, Nigel Jenkins, Robert Minhinnick and Gwyneth Lewis.

Every decade of the century is featured, as is almost every part of Wales – urban, industrial and rural. Wales now has a rich, vibrant and varied literature in English and this anthology reflects it in a comprehensive, authoritative and lively way.

'This anthology is a wonderful compendium of good poems and poets worth meeting, many worth returning to again and again.'
– *New Welsh Review*

'a landmark in the English language writing of Wales.'
– *Cambria*

PB / £20.00
978-1-902638-88-1

LETTERS FROM WALES: MEMORIES AND ENCOUNTERS IN LITERATURE AND LIFE

Sam Adams

Foreword by Michael Schmidt

Edited and with an introduction by Jonathan Edwards

'Since 1996, the 'letters' have been appearing in *PN Review*, one of the most highly-regarded English literary magazines. A case can be made that they are the most significant and sustained attempt during this period to present Welsh writing to an audience throughout the UK and beyond. Their collection for the first time in this volume offers a fascinating cross-section of Welsh literary culture during this period.'
– Jonathan Edwards

'This is a huge book which serves to demonstrate the no less enormous contribution made by Sam Adams to Welsh literary life… Adams is consistently the most amiable and urbane of companions, illuminating and entertaining as he intelligently surveys the world of letters from a Welsh perspective.'
– *Nation. Cymru*

'In these columns, as impressive for their depth as they are for their intellectual breadth, Adams analyses the work of acclaimed Welsh writers such as Gillian Clarke, R. S. Thomas, and Rhian Edwards with scholarly panache'
– *Buzz Magazine*

HB / £20.00
978-1-914595-07-3